The World is Your Oyster

Dr Shirley Lau
MBBS, DCH, DTCH, MSc(MCH), MD, FRACGP

Dr Kimberly Tin
BSc(Hons), MBBCh(UK)

A catalogue record for this book is available from the National Library of Australia

Copyright © 2023 by Shirley Lau and Kimberly Tin

All rights reserved. No part of this book may be reproduced or transmitted in any form or by any means, electronic or mechanical, including photocopying, recording, or by any information storage and retrieval system, without permission in writing from the copyright owner.

Publisher:
Inspiring Publishers
P.O. Box 159, Calwell, ACT Australia 2905
Email: inspiringpublisher.com
http://www.inspiringpublishers.com

National Library of Australia Cataloguing-in-Publication entry

Author: Shirley Lau and Kimberly Tin

Title: **The World is Your Oyster**

ISBN: 978-1-922920-53-9 (Print)
ISBN: 978-1-922920-54-6 (eBook)
ISBN: 978-1-922920-55-3 (PDF eBook)

Dedication

Shirley Lau:
for husband Tin Htoon and son Shai Wan

Kimberly Tin:
for father Tin Htoon,
brother Shai Wan and partner Nihal

Foreword

From one adventurer to another ..... having been an Olympian for the Italian sailing team in 1956, and later to have circumnavigated the world in 1983, I believe The World is Your Oyster is a refreshing read with practical and useful travelling tips.

Shirley is an amazing, empathetic doctor, adding credibility to the advice she gives and fascination to the tales she and her daughter tell.

Happy and safe travels,

Luciano Sandrin
Olympian and Adventurer

Acknowledgments

Special thanks to Mr Luciano Sandrin, Olympian and an Adventurer, Thanking also to Jason Sandrin, son of Luciano.

Also would like to thank Demita and her work team Jaime, Anita, Ben, Emily and Emme who work at Office Works for helping me print our photos.

Finally, thanks to the Self Publishing Group Australia, to all the Team members who are involved in our book.

About the Authors

This is a truly unique travel book written by a mother and daughter who have travelled extensively, sharing their experience and giving tips and advice on travelling.

Shirley Lau MBBS, DCH, DTCH, MSc (MCH), MD, FRACGP
Was also a Fellow of the Academy of Medicine, Singapore, FAMS

Shirley, also known as Myint Myint Thein, is a medical doctor who has travelled extensively to many countries over the past 40 years. She has not only travelled for leisure but also worked in many developed and developing countries, bringing with her a wealth of experience in post-graduate medical training and degrees in Paediatrics, Maternal and Child Health, Women's Health, Public Health, and Family Medicine (General Practice).

Shirley has worked in numerous hospitals and clinics as a clinician and academician, including at the National University of Singapore for over 10 years. She has published 20 research papers in international and local Singapore journals. Additionally, she has worked for the World Health Organisation (WHO) and served as a short-term consultant for the United Nations International Children's Emergency Fund (UNICEF). Furthermore, she has worked at travel-accredited clinics, taught medical students, general practitioners, and public health students taking up their master's degrees for over 35 years. She co-authored a book titled Asian Child Care, published in 1997 in Singapore. In 2002, she co-authored books on health education for primary school children, including course books and workbooks for Grade 4, 5, and 6 in Singapore. Shirley received the Singapore Medical Journal Best Research Paper Award First Prize in 2005 for her research paper on childhood injuries in Singapore, titled, 'Knowledge attitudes and practices of childhood Injuries and their prevention by primary caregivers in Singapore.' This research paper was one of the papers she completed for her doctorate.

Shirley has travelled using different modes of transport, such as air, cruises, trains, road trips, coaches, cars, and walking tours. She has travelled with her family, solo, and for work, balancing her career and raising children while travelling for the past 40 years.

Kimberly Tin BSc (Hons) MBBCh (UK)

Kimberly Tin, Shirley's daughter, has also travelled extensively. She has travelled with her family and alone, including school camps and trips with friends. Born in Singapore, Kimberly studied at Nan Yang Primary school in Singapore and later completed her secondary education at Toorak College, Mt Eliza, Victoria, Australia. After finishing her VCE Year 12, Kimberly earned her Bachelor of Science degree from the University of Melbourne. She was an Honours student at the Florey Institute of Neuroscience in Melbourne, Australia. In 2018, she moved to the United Kingdom to pursue a degree in Medicine, studying at Swansea University from 2018 to 2022. She has since graduated in 2022 and is currently a Junior Doctor at Dorset County Hospital, Dorchester, England, United Kingdom.

Kimberly has one research paper published in 2018, following her Honours degree thesis in Melbourne, Australia.

Contents

Introduction 13

Chapter 1: Destinations 19

Chapter 2: The Purpose of Travelling 47

Chapter 3: Special Interests 93

Chapter 4: Different Modes of Transport 104

Chapter 5: An Interlude: Kimberly's Experience in Travelling
(Child and Young Adult's Perspective) 132

Chapter 6: Preparation for Travel 153

Chapter 7: Health Issues and Prevention 158

Chapter 8: Miscellaneous 163

Chapter 9: My Personal Experience of Different Countries and
What I Still Want to Do. 168

Chapter 10: Summary 170

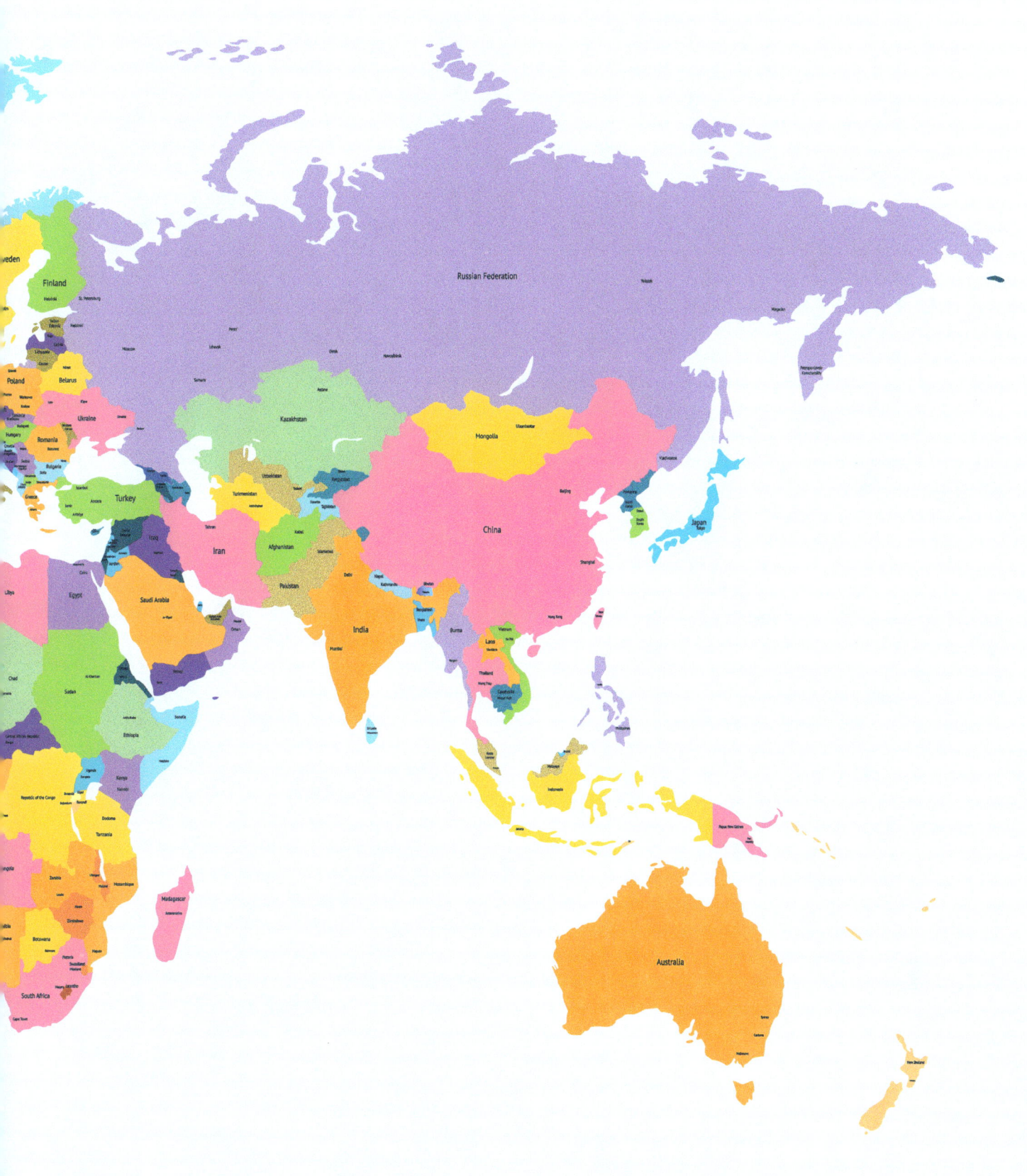

Introduction

From the tender age of five or six, I've nurtured a love and passion for travel. I was born and raised in Burma, now known as Myanmar. My paternal grandparents hailed from Guangzhou, China.

Throughout my childhood, during school holidays, my parents would take my siblings and me to the hilly regions of the Shan State, Kalaw, and Taungyi. We traveled by train, and we also visited the famous and picturesque Inle Lake. Our adventures extended to Ngapali Beach, situated in the north-western part of Myanmar. We flew there, a journey of about 45 minutes from our home in the capital city, Rangoon, which is now called Yangon. Our trips to the beach would vary, sometimes lasting a day, other times stretching to one or two weeks.

As a child, I spent a lot of time poring over world maps, fascinated by the different continents and countries. For a time, I naively thought that, like Australia, Africa was one country. This interest in other countries has never waned; it continues to fuel my desire to travel to various countries, cities, and places, both within Myanmar and abroad.

In my teenage years, my siblings and I participated in competitive swimming and sailing. We trained in the Ngapali Sea and the Mergui Archipelago at Mali Kyun (Mali Island), at the northern end of the archipelago, in preparation for international events. We spent about one to two months there, awed by the stunning beauty of the beach, rocks, lagoons, and waterfalls. Swimming in a lagoon fed by a waterfall remains a vivid memory. The area was rich with beautiful birds, including hornbills, egrets, kingfishers, and eagles. The Mergui Archipelago remains one of the planet's most pristine and unspoiled destinations.

After graduating and becoming a doctor and medical practitioner, I spent four and a half years working in Mandalay, an ancient capital of the Royal Kingdom and a World Heritage Site area in Myanmar. During this period, I visited Bagan, one of Myanmar's most frequented tourist cities, multiple times. Situated not far from Mandalay, Bagan is an ancient city and a UNESCO World Heritage Site in the Mandalay Region of Myanmar, known for its beautiful pagodas and temples. Sagaing, a city near Bagan, offers an incredible boat trip along the famous Irrawaddy River, revealing the temples and pagodas from a unique perspective.

While working as a tutor in the Physiology and Paediatrics Departments of Mandalay University's Medicine Department, I accompanied 100 outstanding students awarded by the government on a journey. As part of a medical team, consisting of two doctors and two nurses, I travelled along an overnight land route from Prome, across the River Irrawaddy on a "Z" craft carrier boat, and then through the Taung Goke pass on four coaches. Each coach carried a member of the medical team, ensuring immediate medical assistance if needed. Our journey included stops at various places, crossing two streams, and culminating at Ngapali Beach.

The trip was extraordinary. I chronicled the experience in an article for the Mandalay Institute of Medicine's annual magazine, which I titled 'A Glorious Fortnight'. I discovered that road trips could be just as enjoyable as air or rail journeys.

In 1978, I received a scholarship and assessment scheme in paediatrics for postgraduate training in the United Kingdom. This opportunity was available to young doctors under 30 years old. I moved to the UK in early 1979 and stayed there for eight years, undergoing six years of hospital training in paediatrics and two years in community paediatrics. I earned a Diploma in Child Health (DCH) and a Diploma in Tropical Child Health (DTCH). Simultaneously, I pursued a Maternal and Child Health Master's course at the University of London, while working and taking exams.

During my time in the UK, I extensively traveled to numerous European countries, the United States, Mexico, Canada, and a few Asian countries. In 1980/81, I spent about five months in India, conducting research for my Master's degree at the Child In Need Institute in Daulatpur, a village overseeing 49 others in West Bengal, situated 28 kilometers from Calcutta. After my work in three selected villages and assistance at the clinic, I embarked on a tour to New Delhi, Agra, Jaipur, Varanasi, River Ganges, Bodh Gaya, Sarnath, Kushinaga, and crossed the India-Nepal border to visit Lumbini, the birthplace of Lord Buddha. This was an incredible experience.

Throughout my research study, I visited homes in the selected West Bengal villages, examining children under five years old, providing advice and treatment, assessing mothers' knowledge on child care, immunizations, and child safety injury prevention. Every family I visited extended their hospitality by offering me food or drink. They were friendly, respectful, and showed immense kindness - memories I cherish.

After my eight-year stint in the UK, I moved to Singapore and worked as a lecturer at the National University of Singapore for 11 years. During that time, I earned my FAMS (fellowship degree) and a Doctor of Medicine degree.(Doctorate degree).

I chose not to follow the traditional path of studying when young, then settling into a career and starting a family, with travel reserved only for retirement at the age of 60 or 65. I often reasoned that by retirement age, one's physical fitness might have declined, making travel less enjoyable. This realization has become more evident as I've grown older.

INTRODUCTION

In my youth, I combined study with travel during school holidays. While in the UK for postgraduate studies, I worked, saved money, and took two to three-week travel breaks intermittently.

Nowadays, many young people take a gap year to travel after their A-level or VCE Year 12 exams in Australia, before starting university or work. During this gap year, they travel overseas, sometimes with friends or parents, or visit relatives if they've migrated from another country. They work for a short period, save money, and continue to travel. Some receive financial support from their parents.

During my time working in Australia as a general practitioner and travel medicine specialist, I met many young people taking gap years to work and travel in European countries. Some worked on farms or orchards for a few months, saved money, and then continued their journeys. I encountered a few who traveled overseas to house-sit for families on vacation. They saved their earnings and continued to travel upon the families' return.

While traveling when young can be beneficial, it's equally important not to neglect further education. Striking a balance between travel, education, and work is key, especially given that you need to earn money to travel. I also advocate for regular holidays and short breaks from work every one to two years for those over 30. If time and finances allow, a short break every year can be fruitful, reducing stress and enhancing enjoyment for you and your family.

I have contemplated writing this book for over 25 years and have composed some chapters in the past 15 years. In 2011, while traveling with my daughter to the UK and Europe on rail journeys using a Euro Rail Pass, I watched a television interview with an author. This English lady, who was around my age, if not older, had written several books. When asked why she still wrote books in this modern era, she responded that she loved books and believed many people still enjoyed reading them, even with the availability of e-books and online resources. This inspired me to complete my book.

Over the 40 years since I began traveling overseas, it has become increasingly enjoyable and convenient. However, safety has become a concern in some parts of the world due to wars, natural disasters, and political unrest. The recent Covid-19 pandemic and ensuing lockdowns have further complicated travel. Despite this, the beauty of travel lies in the array of transport modes and destinations available to suit everyone's preferences.

In this modern age, those with time and money can enjoy comfortable trips. In this book, I aim to provide useful information for both novice and seasoned travelers. Even the most experienced travelers may discover places or activities they've missed and may wish to revisit these cities or countries. Over the years, certain sites have disappeared, and new ones have emerged, like the Modern 7 Natural Wonders of the World, such as Halong Bay in Hanoi, Vietnam; Table Mountain in Cape Town, South Africa; and Jeju Island in South Korea.

The World is Your Oyster

During my travels, particularly on cruises, I've met individuals who've embarked on numerous cruises, ranging from short one-week trips to repeat world cruises. These cruises typically include one or two-day stops in various cities or countries. For instance, I met a couple who visited Beijing, China, but only had a day to explore, so they chose to see the Forbidden City and Tiananmen Square, missing out on the Great Wall.

Some may not be interested in visiting famous walls, and while I have a penchant for natural beauty, I wouldn't prioritize walls on my bucket list either. However, having visited the Berlin Wall in 1980 and the Great Wall in 2016, I can attest that even these man-made wonders have their own unique beauty. The Berlin Wall, a straight wall adorned with graffiti, divided East and West Berlin. In contrast, the Great Wall, stretching 13,000 miles across mountains, is an awe-inspiring sight, with multiple sections available for tourists to climb. I believe that it's important to visit and appreciate such man-made wonders.

For those seeking a more in-depth exploration of a country or city, I recommend flying into that country or disembarking from your ship and spending one to two weeks exploring. I aim to provide valuable advice, tips, and share my personal travel experiences throughout this book.

I plan to provide information on various modes of transport, catering to those who wish to spend several weeks touring large countries like India, China, the USA, UK, Canada, and Australia. You could fly into the country and then take domestic flights, embark on train journeys, drive, or even take coach tours.

I've had the pleasure of experiencing different modes of transport. The idea for this book came to me years ago when I was on a cruise. Several of my medical colleagues confessed they found the idea of cruising boring, assuming the ship would be sailing constantly. In reality, I found cruising holidays incredibly enjoyable. I'll delve deeper into this topic in the chapter on modes of travel. Once you've experienced a cruise, you'll find yourself yearning for more. It's a stress-free mode of travel where your hotel travels with you, eliminating the need to constantly pack and unpack your luggage or lug it around at different ports.

On luxury ships, there's an entire floor dedicated to shops where you can find unique items or gifts not commonly available in regular city or country shops. I often purchase presents for birthdays and other occasions during these cruises, leaving my friends amazed at my unique finds. Airplane in-flight catalogues also offer some special items not usually available in standard shops.

In this book, you'll find useful travel information that isn't typically included in other travel guides, such as health issues, disease prevention, necessary vaccines, medical conditions to be checked, preventive measures to take before travelling, and what to avoid while travelling.

Introduction

What makes this book unique is that my daughter, who recently turned 28, will also contribute, sharing her own travel experiences. Our writing styles differ; mine is more serious and factual, while hers is light-hearted and humorous.

We, a mother and daughter duo who love travelling, aim to provide you with valuable information to aid your holiday planning, or preparations to study or work in another country. The combined insights from an adult traveller and a younger perspective will be valuable for many travellers.

We've included many photos, primarily our own, understanding that text-heavy books can be unappealing to readers. However, books filled solely with photos and illustrations, while visually appealing, often lack substantial information. Unfortunately, we've lost some photos of certain countries and places we've visited, so we've only included the photos we still have.

This book is distinctive, as most travel books are written by non-medical individuals. When a health professional writes a travel guide, it tends to focus heavily on health. This book, however, is intended for those wishing to see the world, follow their dreams, and tick off their bucket list items. We provide essential information and share personal experiences to ensure your travels are safe, healthy, enjoyable, and fulfilling.

Bon voyage!
Shirley Lau

Chapter One
Destinations

The World Is Your Oyster, You can do anything or go anywhere you want to You can take the opportunities that life has to offer.

Destinations are places where people make a special trip, be it holidays, adventures or for work. There are many places worth going to but some places not many people can go or climb like the top of Mt. Everest. Even climbing to base camp is no easy matter.

There are also many sporting events which are held every few years, such as the Olympic Games or the yearly Australian Open for tennis or the World Cup for football.

People have different interests and in this chapter we will be writing and giving the different destinations that people would like to visit.

Dream Destinations

Dream destinations are places, cities, countries that people dream of visiting.

Must-see Destinations

Must-see destinations are places or locations that a lot of people like, can be very famous places, historical sites, or spots of immense beauty, landscapes, fascinating and sensational cities. These places can easily be reached by many people. They also include the natural or man-made wonders.

Spiritual Destinations

Certain special places move us at a profound level with a kind of inner beauty that puts us in direct touch with the spirit.

It may be a temple, a church, or any site with the ambience of ancient sacred traditions.

Such places are worth taking the trouble to visit. They add meaning to our lives, awakening a sense of awe, beauty, or tranquility.

THE WORLD IS YOUR OYSTER

Shirley's Dream Destinations:

1. **Africa (for safaris):** From a very young age, I wanted to visit Africa to go on a safari to see animals in their natural habitat.
2. **Nepal:** To see the Himalayas, especially Mt. Everest.
3. **Japan:** To see Mt. Fuji, which is different from the Himalayas as it is only one mountain. Also, to experience the cherry blossom season during the end of March and the first week of April when the whole country is in bloom with cherry blossoms.
4. **Waterfalls:** Waterfalls are another of my dream destinations. To see Victoria Falls, Niagara Falls, and other waterfalls.
5. **Cruise on QE2:** When I was working at the National University of Singapore, a professor colleague went on a cruise on QE2 for two months. When he told me before he went, I wanted to go on that ship, and my dream was to go on that famous cruise later.
6. **Egypt:** My dream was to see the Great Pyramid and to go on a cruise on the River Nile.
7. **Northern Lights:** I wanted to see the Northern Lights. My dream was to visit Norway or Iceland during winter. You will see the Northern Lights more during winter or autumn.
8. **French Polynesia, Tahiti, and Bora Bora:** When I was a child and watched the movie Mutiny on the Bounty starring the famous actor Marlon Brando, my dream was to visit the ship location Tahiti.

Kimberly's Dream Destinations:

1. **Disneyland Holiday Tours:** Since childhood, she has always wanted to visit Disneyland tours in many countries after visiting Disneyland in the USA when she was two.
2. **China:** After studying the history of China in school, Kimberly wanted to visit China to see the Forbidden City, Tiananmen Square, the Terracotta Warriors, and the Great Wall of China.
3. **France:** Wants to visit Paris.
4. **USA:** To visit New York and may want to work in New York.
5. **Norway, Iceland:** To see the fjords and also the Northern Lights.
6. **Tennis Grand Slams:** Kimberly has been in Australia for 13-14 years, and she has gone with her mum to the Australian Tennis Open for many years. Her dream is also to visit other venues of tennis opens, such as the French Open, Wimbledon, and the US Open.

Destinations

Some dream destinations that many people dream of visiting:

1. **Stratford-Upon-Avon:** Shakespeare's birthplace and a charming English town.
2. **London:** England's great city and the world's most popular tourist destination.
3. **New York City:** America's popular urban center and a favorite among many tourists. Also known as 'the City That Never Sleeps'.
4. **Sydney Opera House:** Great architecture.
5. Mornington Peninsula and Great Ocean Road, Victoria.
6. **Great Barrier Reef:** Queensland, one of the world's natural wonders.
7. **Rajasthan:** The largest state in India, famous for many cultural attractions, such as the beautiful temples in the city of Jaipur.
8. French Polynesia, Tahiti, Bora Bora.
9. **Alaska:** Visitors thrill at the wildlife consisting of sea lions, whales, bald eagles, glaciers, cliffs, and Glacier Bay.
10. **Masai Mara:** A natural safari location in Kenya. One of the most famous and important wildlife conservation and wilderness areas in Africa, renowned for its exceptional populations of lion, leopard, cheetah, and bush elephant.
11. **Orient Express:** Venice Simplon Orient Express, from London to Paris or from Paris to London. Famous rail travel.
12. **Victoria Falls:** Located in Zambia and Zimbabwe. One of the Seven Natural Wonders of the World.
13. **Cairo, Egypt:** The Great Pyramid, the only one left amongst the Seven Wonders of the Ancient World.
14. **The Northern Lights:** Can be seen in Norway, Sweden, Finland, and Iceland.

Must-See Destinations

Must-see destinations are places or locations that a lot of people like to visit and see. They can be very famous places, historical sites, world heritage sites, immense beauty, landscapes, fascinating and sensational cities. These places can easily be reached by many people. They can go for holidays or, when they go for work in a country, they will go to nearby places to these popular famous must-see destinations. Must-see destinations include natural and man-made wonders.

THE WORLD IS YOUR OYSTER

Some examples of must-see destinations:

1. USA - Hawaii, Niagara Falls, Empire State Building, Statue of Liberty, The Grand Canyon, and Yosemite

Statue of Liberty, New York USA

DESTINATIONS

Yosemeti Park

The World is Your Oyster

Shirley in front of the White House Washington.

2. **Canada -** The Rocky Mountains and the Ontario side of Niagara Falls
3. **United Kingdom -** London, Oxford, Stonehenge, and Buckingham Palace

Stonehenge, United Kingdom

DESTINATIONS

Buckingham Palace, London UK

London, UK

Destinations

4. France - Paris, Eiffel Tower, The Louvre Museum, and Versailles. The charming countryside of Provence is also a must-see destination.

5. Italy Colosseum, Trevi Fountain, Venice, Vatican City, The Last Supper painting
6. Spain Barcelona, La Sagrada Familia,
7. Germany. Black Forest, Railroad along River Rhine, Berlin Wall
8. Croatia, Dubrovnik
9. Poland, Krakow which is absolutely beautiful
10. Austria Vienna and Salzburg birth place of famous Mozart

11. Czech Republic, Prague, the capital city is bisected by the Vlita River. The Charles bridge is lined withstatues of Catholic saints.
12. Hungary, Budapest, Parlament House,Museum and The Danube River.

Danube cruise

Budapest museum on Danube

DESTINATIONS

5. **Switzerland -** The Swiss Alps, ski resorts, and hiking trails. Swiss watches and chocolates are world-renowned.
6. **Sweden -** Stockholm, spot the Northern Lights in Swedish Lapland, and ABBA (band), "Mamma Mia." ABBA The Museum is located on the Island of Djurgarden.
7. **Norway -** Northern lights, Tromso can see more than other cities, and fjords.

Norway, Thromso, Dog Sledding

16. **Iceland -** tourist spot to see the Northern lights
17. **Russia -** St. Petersburg, a Russian port city on the Baltic Sea. It is very beautiful and has the Bronze Horseman, Church of the Savior on Spilled Blood, Saint Hermitage Museum (St. Petersburg's most popular visitor attraction and one of the world's largest and most prestigious museums), and canals.

The World is Your Oyster

St Petersburg Church of the Savior on the Spilled Blood

18. **China** - Forbidden City, Tiananmen Square, The Great Wall of China, Terracotta Warriors, Yangtze River (the longest river in Asia, the third longest in the world, and the longest river in the world to flow entirely within one country).

The Great Wall of China

DESTINATIONS

Teracotta Warriors, Xian, China

19. **India -** New Delhi, Taj Mahal, Agra, Jaipur, The Golden Triangle (New Delhi, Agra, and Jaipur), Varanasi, River Ganges, and Kashmi

Maha Bodhi Temple Bodh Gaya, India

THE WORLD IS YOUR OYSTER

At historical Nalanda University India 1981
Shirley and a Nun travelled for about 2 months in India

20. **Singapore** - Jewel, Gardens by the Bay, Botanic Garden, Sentosa Island, Marina Bay Sands (Singapore's famous luxury hotel), and Singapore Zoo Night Safari (the world's first night zoo.

DESTINATIONS

Marina Bay Sands Hotel Singapore

21. Malaysia - Penang, Langkawi, and Borneo Island, which is split into three countries, Malaysia, Indonesia, and Brunei. It is the home of orangutans, rainforests, and wildlife.
22. Thailand - Bangkok, Chiang Mai, The Golden Triangle (Thailand, Burma, and Laos), Emerald Temple, and floating markets.
23. Burma, now called Myanmar, has many beautiful places and sites to visit. Not many people have visited Myanmar. Shwedagon Pagoda is the world's most beautiful temple and the most sacred Buddhist pagoda in Myanmar. It is believed to contain relics of the four previous Buddhas and has eight strands of hair from the head of

Lord Buddha Gautama. Other places to visit in Myanmar include Mandalay, the last royal kingdom with a palace and moat, the World Heritage Site Bagan with 3,500 ancient Buddhist pagodas and many temples, Shan State, Inle Lake, and the Mergui Archipelago.

Inya Lake in Yangon Myanma

24. Indonesia is known for Bali, a beautiful and highly visited tourist destination. Other places to visit in Indonesia include the iconic and historic Buddhist temple Borobudur, many volcanoes, the Kintamani Tour, and lovely islands with beautiful landscapes and hot springs.
25. The Philippines is known for Manila's colonial heritage and being a Pacific Rim archipelago with rugged mountains and famed dive sites.
26. Laos has Luang Prabang, a World Heritage site, and Kuang Si Falls, which tumble through the jungle about 29 km from Luang Prabang and are among the area's most attractive waterfalls, combining a dramatic drop and pools. Pak Ou Caves is another religious destination in Laos overlooking the Mekong River. They are the two caves on the west side of the Mekong River, about 2 hours upstream from the center of Luang Prabang and are frequently visited by tourists. The site is spiritual, with mini carved Buddhas inside caves.

DESTINATIONS

Kuang Si waterfalls Lauang Prabang, Laos

Mekong River, Laos

THE WORLD IS YOUR OYSTER

Mekong River Laos

27. Japan is is one of the most famous and well-liked Asian countries. There are many places to visit in Japan, including Tokyo with many attractions like Tokyo Disneyland, Mt. Fuji, Kobe, Nara, Kyoto during Cherry blossom season and the Shinkansan train journey.
28. South Korea has Seoul, Everland theme park, and Jeju Island.
29. Australia has many beautiful areas and attractions. In Victoria, there is Melbourne and the Great Ocean Road. The Mornington Peninsula is also one of the most beautiful areas and seaside locations in Australia, as well as Phillip Island. In New South Wales, there is Sydney with the Sydney Harbour and Opera House, and the Blue Mountains. Queensland has the Great Barrier Reef, the world's largest coral reef system that hosts thousands of marine species, as well as Cairns, a gateway to the reef and tropical Daintree Rainforest. Brisbane, the capital of Queensland, is flanked by the surfing beaches of the Gold and Sunshine Coast Uluru.or Ayres rock in Central Australia nearest town is Alice Springs. Adelaide is where the famous train, The Ghan, starts.

Destinations

Uluru, Australia

30. New Zealand has Auckland and beautiful islands north and south of the country.
31. French Polynesia has Tahiti, a large French Polynesian island with the capital of Papeete, as well as black sand beaches, volcanoes, and museums. Bora Bora is another breathtakingly beautiful small island in French Polynesia, northwest of Tahiti in the South Pacific. You will be surprised to see any place on Earth with so much beauty concentrated in one spot. It is a small lush island surrounded by tiny islets fringed with sparkling white sand and a blue lagoon surrounded by a barrier coral reef. In the heart of the small island is an extinct volcano with its one peak Mount Otemanu. From the plane, you can see the magnificent view of Bora Bora.

The World is Your Oyster

Bora Bora French Polynesia

32. Africa - Kenya's Maasai Mara is one of the world's greatest safari destinations, famous for its exceptional populations of lions, African leopards, cheetahs, and African bush elephants. It's also an important wildlife conservation and wilderness area in Africa, with a rich cultural heritage. In African safaris, the Big 5 are the most sought after: lions, leopards, rhinos, elephants, and African buffaloes. Lake Nakuru is home to about 40% of the world's Flamingos forming a rim at the coast of the lake.

DESTINATIONS

Lake Nakuru, Kenya

The World is Your Oyster

Safaris, Animals

Destinations

33. Africa – Tanzania is home to the world-famous Serengeti Safari and Mount Kilimanjaro.
34. South Africa – Johannesburg offers the Kruger Safari and Sun City, while Cape Town Boasts Table Mountain one of the modern Natural Wonders.

South Africa, Cape Town

35. Africa – Egypt is known for the Great Pyramid and the River Nile.
36. Africa – Zambia and Zimbabwe are two African countries known for world famous Victoria Fall.

Victoria Falls bridge crosses the Zambezi River

37. Africa – Seychelles offers beautiful beaches, coral reefs and giant Aldabra tortoises
38. Africa – Mauritius is an island with dream beaches and turquoise water, considered a Popular tourist attraction.it also boasts the Chamarel Seven Coloured Earth Geopark

Destinations

39. Turkey offers Istanbul's Hagia Sophia, Cappadocia's Rose and Love Valley, and Ephesus.

40. Holland Amsterdam In Spring beautiful Tulips,, Windmills and clogs

Spiritual Destinations

Spiritual destinations are important to visit regardless of your religion or personal preferences. Certain special places move us at a profound level with a kind of inner beauty that puts us in direct touch with the spirit. It may be a temple, a church, or an ambience of sacred traditions. Such places are worth taking the trouble to visit, as they add meaning to our lives, awakening a sense of awe, beauty, and tranquility.

THE WORLD IS YOUR OYSTER

I respect all religions and have been to some religious places, but mostly I have no photos. Here are some spiritual destinations to consider:

1. **Jerusalem** - capital of Israel, is one of the oldest cities in the world and is considered holy for the three major Abrahamic religions - Judaism, Christianity, and Islam. It contains religious structures such as Western Wall, the Dome of the Rock, and al-Aqsa Mosque. For Christians, according to the New Testament, Jerusalem was the city to which Jesus was brought up as a child to be presented at the Temple and to attend the festival of Passover. According to the gospels, Jesus Christ preached and healed in Jerusalem, especially in the courts of the Temple.

2. **Bethlehem** - the birthplace of Jesus, which is 10 km south of Jerusalem.

3. **Churches and Cathedrals in Rome, Vatican City** - a city-state surrounded by Rome, Italy, is the headquarters of the Roman Catholic Church. It is home to the Pope and a trove of iconic art and architecture. St Peter's Basilica, in Vatican City, holds a unique position in the Christian world and is the greatest of all churches of Christendom. I have travelled to Italy many times and, in my younger days, I saw Pope John Paul II coming out and giving a sermon just outside St Peter's Basilica Cathedral.

4. **Buddhism - India** - Lord Buddha's Footsteps - from birth in Lumbini to teachings and preachings, enlightenment at Bodhgaya and Kushinaga, and his death at 80 years old.

Buddha's teachings

DESTINATIONS

At Bodh Gaya India

At Bodh Gaya inside the temple

At Kushinaga Lord Buddha passed away at 80 years age

5. **Hinduism:**
   Varanasi: Varanasi is considered a sacred place for many religions such as Hinduism and Jainism. Many Buddhists also visit Varanasi because Sarnath, the place where Lord Buddha gave his first sermon to his five disciples after his enlightenment, is very close by. Both foreign tourists and locals seeking peace and spiritual clarity gather on the banks of the River Ganges to queue up at various temples every day to seek blessings and recite prayers.
   Sri Lanka: Sri Lanka is home to a lot of Buddhists, with a Bodhi tree sapling brought from India and tooth relics of Lord Buddha.

6. **Haj - Annual Haj Pilgrimage for Muslims to Mecca:**
   Mecca is situated in a desert valley in Western Saudi Arabia and is considered Islam's holiest city because it is the birthplace of the Prophet Mohammed and the religion. A pilgrimage to Mecca is obligatory for all Muslims, and millions of people flock to the city every year to pay their respects. Mecca is home to the Kaaba, a building that is the center of Islam's most sacred mosque, Al-Masjid al-Haram, and is the most sacred Muslim site in the world.

Chapter Two:
The Purpose of Travelling

Work

People often work in different countries, particularly those who work for large companies or organizations such as engineers, IT professionals, builders, medical professionals working for organizations like World Health Organization, UNICEF, United Nations, Doctors Without Borders, medical doctors and nurses, and those working in academics such as lecturers and professors who visit many countries for conferences. Politicians also frequently visit different countries for work-related purposes while they are in office, such as presidents, prime ministers, and various ministers.

When I was working as a lecturer at the National University of Singapore, I visited many countries for staff exchange programs, such as the United States of America (Johns Hopkins University), Japan (Kobe, Nara, Tokyo), and Denver, Colorado, USA for Child Development and Denver Developmental Screening Test training. Later, I conducted research with the DDST-S (Singapore version) back in Singapore. I also went to many countries for conferences, presenting my research papers in Dallas, Texas, USA, Montreal, Canada, Johannesburg, South Africa, Thailand, the Philippines, Indonesia, Vietnam, and Nepal and South Korea.

In Singapore, Child Safety Centre, K K Hospital

Symposium on Health and Women at Work, in Singapore

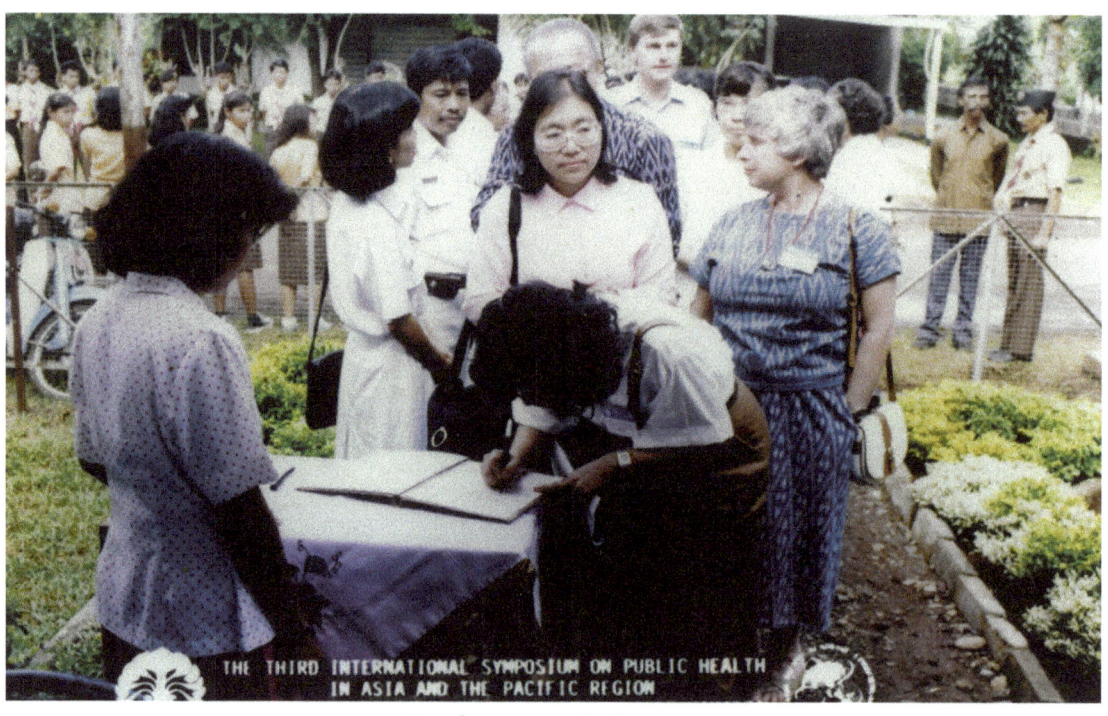
Conference in Indonesia

The Purpose of Travelling

In South Korea, World Health Organisation, Conference 2002

In South Africa, Johannesburg 1997 conference

In Mexico, I was in the villages for 3 months

After conference in Vienna I went to the Mozart Museum

The Purpose of Travelling

In Vienna, Austria

Working in UK 1979

THE WORLD IS YOUR OYSTER

Working in United Kingdom from 1979 to 1986

The Purpose of Travelling

In Japan, Railway Station

In Japan, Kobe 1987 Staff Exchange Programme

At Santa Fe Conference in USA

When I had to go to other countries for staff exchange programs, the trips were longer, such as three months to John Hopkins in the USA and one month in Japan. I went to Hawaii for about two months to conduct research. When I attended conferences, the conference period was only about a week, and then they usually had post-conference tours. I did join a few of these tours, such as the Navajo land tour for a week after the Santa Fe conference in the USA. It was an amazing trip, visiting tribal parks, historical sites, and national monuments with beautiful landscapes.

Post conference tour after Santa Fe Conference

The Purpose of Travelling

In Malaysia

What I want to convey about my work-related trips is that after finishing my work in a particular city or country, I would take my own leave from work for about two weeks. If the country was big and I had not been there before, I would visit other famous places in that country. If the country was small and I had already been there, I would go to a nearby country for a week and then fly back home. I did mostly like that with work. When you go for work, you are paid for the trip, so it is good to spend one or two weeks after work to visit famous places or your dream destinations if they are there. This way, you do not need to spend extra money and time to come back later. If you like the place very much, you can plan a holiday with your family later.

A lot of people I know go to work for a certain time period and when work finishes, they go back home straight away. If the work period is three to six months, it is quite long, and the person usually misses their family and goes home immediately.

Holidays

Short or long holidays, one or multiple countries, going on holidays with family or friends is very beneficial. It is recommended to go on overseas holidays every two to three years for two to three weeks. If in a big country like Australia, one can visit other states or in countries like India and China, other areas of the country can be explored once a year. In the UK, it is easy to visit Paris with just a rail journey, while in the US, there are many places to visit during school holidays. Canada also has many holiday destinations.

Holidays can be taken alone or with friends, and some people even make friends during their holiday. Youngsters may prefer whirlwind tours to six or seven countries in two weeks, which can be good for first-time travelers. However, people's interests differ, so it is difficult to say which is the best. It also depends on age, financial status, and who you are traveling with - alone, with family or friends. For holidays with family or friends, it is preferable to travel to one or two countries for two to three weeks.

While holidays are enjoyable, it is important for young people to prioritize their education by taking holidays during school holidays. For people working, it is good to take short breaks to relax from work, but it is also essential to continue working and saving money.

THE PURPOSE OF TRAVELLING

My holiday photos

At Las Vegas Disneyland

The World is Your Oyster

At Las Vegas Disneyland USA with son and daughter

The Purpose of Travelling

With son Shai Wan and daughter Kimberly in USA

The World is Your Oyster

Berlin Wall

Shirley in front of Berlin Wall 1981

The World is Your Oyster

Shirley at Trevi Fountain, Rome, Italy Coin Toss

The Purpose of Travelling

Daughter and son at Terracotta Warriors Xi An

China Beijing with son and daughter

THE WORLD IS YOUR OYSTER

Beijing Tiananmen Square, China with my son and daughter

At The Great Wall, China

Mt Eliza, Victoria Australia

In front of Crab Apple Tree 2022 September, Mt Eliza

Tulips in our garden Mt Eliza

The Purpose of Travelling

Mt Eliza Beach boxes

Beautiful, Sunsets

The World is Your Oyster

Stonehenge UK with family, husband and children

London, United Kingdom

Niagara Falls Canada 1980

Niagara Falls

The World is Your Oyster

Niagara Falls USA side 2018

Victoria Falls

The Purpose of Travelling

Victoria Falls on bridge connecting Zambia and Zimbabwe

Kuang Si WaterFall in Layong Prabang, Laos

The World is Your Oyster

The Red Sands, Mauritius

In Seychelles

The Purpose of Travelling

With Best Friend April at the Black Forest, Germany 1981

Baden Baden, Black Forest 1981

At Black Forest Germany 1981

The Purpose of Travelling

USA Tour

With Daughter at Uluru Australia

South Africa with Husband Tin Htoon

Cape Town South Africa

Safari, Shirley on the jeep and near the lions

Safari tour, leopard on the tree

Safari tour Africa

THE WORLD IS YOUR OYSTER

Indonesia, Borobudoh

At Bali, Indonesia

The Purpose of Travelling

Borobudoh, Indonesia, 1988

Kintamini Tour Indonesia

The World is Your Oyster

Kintamini Tour, Indonesia, Volcano

China, The Great Wall

The Purpose of Travelling

With daughter Kimberly in Tokyo Japan Cherry Blossom Season

Kimberly and Mum near Mt Fuji

At Taj Mahal, India 2015

The Purpose of Travelling

Kathmandu, Nepal after my WHO conference, key note speaker at the International Symposium on the Girl Child : A Neglected Majority, 14th Dec 1990.

The World is Your Oyster

In Pattaya Bay Thailand 1985

Great Ocean Road, Twelve Apostles Victoria, Australia

The Purpose of Travelling

Transit Countries/Cities:

When traveling overseas for very long journeys, planes often stop for two to three hours in a country to change planes or for passengers to board the same plane. Passengers are allowed to disembark and spend time in the airport before continuing their journey. I used to never stop over in these countries for a few days, but now that I am older, I stop for a few days to rest. If you have never been to that country or city, it is good to stop over for two to three days and visit the place. For example, if you are flying with Singapore Airlines, you can stop at Singapore for a few days. If you are flying with Emirates Airlines, you can stop for a few days in Dubai.

In Dubai

Dubai, we stayed a few days

Abu Dhabi

The Purpose of Travelling

School Trips:

Many schools organize trips for secondary school children to go to another country with their teachers, where they participate in various activities and voluntary work, spending about a month in a developing country. This is a great opportunity not only to help people and communities in another country but also to develop kindness, helpfulness, and compassion, which will stay with them throughout their adult lives.

Volunteering Work:

Some adults use their free time to do voluntary work in many developing countries. In 1981, when I went to India and was flying to villages in West Bengal, there was a young girl, about 20 years old, sitting next to me on the airplane. We left London, and she was going to Calcutta to do voluntary work for a few months at Mother Teresa's place. I praised her for her good work and for going alone to do voluntary work. When we landed in Calcutta, I had to take a bus to Daulatpur village, which is about 28 km from Calcutta, to go to Child In Need Institute. The institute covers 49 villages, and Daulatpur is the main village where they have young female students doing a six-month course in Maternal and Child Health. For the next one or two months, I went to Mother Teresa's place in Calcutta to see her, but I missed her. They had gone to another place, and at that time, we did not have mobile phones to contact them.

Studying abroad

Many young adults over the age of 18 leave their home country to study in different universities abroad for a few years. It's a great opportunity to learn and gain experience in the UK and the USA. However, many young people who are around 18 or 19 years old may not want to leave their family. After obtaining a Science or Arts degree in their home country, they may choose to pursue other specialties, such as Engineering, Law, or Medicine, in the UK or the USA.

Adventure tours

Safaris, such as the Masai Mara in Kenya and the Serengeti in Tanzania, are popular adventure tours, as well as hiking tours in many countries, trekking, climbing, such as the Base Camp at Mt. Everest or the Swiss Alps, cycling in the country, or cycling tours in Europe. Some groups also travel to places like Antarctica or the Galapagos. One time, a group of doctors was planning a trip, and I wanted to go, but I missed out.

THE WORLD IS YOUR OYSTER

Sporting events

If you're a sports enthusiast, you may want to attend various tournaments and competitions, such as the SEA Games, Asian Games, Commonwealth Games, Olympic Games, Tennis Grand Slams, ATP Tours, WTA Tours, cricket tournaments, football games, World Cup football, basketball, motor racing, sailing, swimming, and cycling, Marathon events.. This will give you the chance to visit different countries while watching your favourite sport.

Myself and my daughter in Australia for many years we have gone to watch Australia Open Grand Slam Tennis for about 10 times.every year we go.Mother and daughter together in Australia for about 14 years.

My favourite tennis star was Roger Federer and have seen him playing at tournaments as well as when he is training at some of the training grounds .

Just before Roger retired a young boy only 18 years old was playing very well, smiling, very humble friendly to everybody and he become my little young star, he is Carlos Alcaraz.

At South Korea 2002 just before the World Cup Football

Tennis Grand Slam Australian Open, Melbourne

US Open Grand Slam Tennis, New York

Chapter Three:
Special Interests

People have different interests, and they want to visit the places that they like, their dream destinations, or their bucket lists.

Historical Destinations

Many people love to visit historical destinations and want to know more about the history of past events and famous historical figures belonging to the past. Studying history helps us understand how events in the past made things the way they are today. With lessons from the past, we not only learn about ourselves and how we came to be, but also develop the ability to avoid mistakes and create better paths for our societies. Visiting historical sites can lead to a deeper engagement with historical events and give us an opportunity to develop a fuller appreciation for those who lived before us. These experiences can be very valuable.

Historical destinations:
1. **Stonehenge, England** - an ancient stone circle located in Wiltshire, England. It is one of the most mysterious and popular tourist destinations in the United Kingdom.

THE WORLD IS YOUR OYSTER

StoneHenge UK

2. Petra, Jordan
3. Machu Picchu, Peru
4. The Colosseum, Rome

Colosseum, Rome, Italy.

Special Interests

Trevi Fountain, Rome, Italy

5. Angkor Wat, Cambodia
6. Taj Mahal, India
7. The Pyramids of Giza, Egypt

8. The Great Wall of China
9. The Forbidden City
10. Leaning Tower of Pisa, Italy

Leaning Tower of Pisa, Italy

Special Interests

11. Acropolis, Athens, Greece
12. Archaeological areas of Pompeii
13. Borobudur temple, Indonesia
14. Palace and gardens of Versailles, France

Art and Culture

People who are curious about the cultures of the world often visit theatres, museums, galleries, and libraries. Some famous museums are:

1. Van Gogh Museum in Amsterdam, the Netherlands
2. Austrian Gallery Belvedere in Vienna, Austria
3. State Hermitage Museum in Saint Petersburg, Russia
4. Tate Britain Art Gallery in London, England
5. The Moscow Kremlin in Moscow, Russia

Art is the creative work of making or doing things that have beauty. It includes painting, sculpture, architecture, music, literature, drama, and dance.

Some of the most famous paintings include the Mona Lisa painting at the Louvre museum in Paris, France and "The Last Supper" painting by Leonardo Da Vinci in Milan's Santa Maria delle Grazie Church, painted between 1495 and 1497. To see the original painting, one must go to Milan, Italy. It is on many people's bucket list and is one of the world's most recognizable and most visited paintings.

What makes this painting so unique is the distinct expressions of each person at the table, including Judas who betrayed Jesus. There were names written at the bottom of the painting. When I visited, each group of twenty people were only allowed to stay for 15 to 20 minutes. I was happy to have seen it, as I had missed it a few years prior when I visited Milan without booking ahead. They would not allow me to enter without a reservation, so my daughter and I booked it before we traveled to ensure we could see it.

Scenery and Great Landscapes

Stunning photographs that inspire and astonish people include rivers, deserts, mountains (such as the Himalayas in Nepal and the Alps in Switzerland), seacoast lines, and the Red Centre of Australia. There are also unique landscapes such as the Coloured Sands in Mauritius and the Coloured Sands on the Isle of Wight in the UK, and treasures from the air, like the Grand Canyon in the USA, and the Great Barrier Reef in Australia. Hot air balloon rides over the Bagan Temples in Myanmar offer a unique perspective.

Seven Natural Wonders of the World

1. Mt Everest in Nepal
2. The Grand Canyon in the USA
3. Victoria Falls in Zambia and Zimbabwe
4. Harbour of Rio de Janeiro in Brazil
5. The Great Barrier Reef in Queensland, Australia
6. The Northern Lights or Aurora Borealis can be seen in Norway, Sweden, Iceland, Greenland, Swedish and Finnish Lapland, Scotland, Siberia, Canada, and Alaska.
7. Paricutin Volcano in Mexico

Seven Wonders of the Ancient World

Only one wonder is left: the Great Pyramid of Egypt.

Man-Made Wonders
1. Golden Gate Bridge in the USA
2. Machu Picchu in Peru
3. Empire State Building in New York, USA
4. Panama Canal - an artificial 82km waterway in Panama that connects the Atlantic and Pacific Oceans and divides North and South America.
5. The Great Wall of China
6. Taj Mahal in India
7. Terracotta Warriors in China

Romantic holidays Honeymoons

Wedding anniversaries
Famous places for these are: Paris, New York, French Polynesia Tahiti, Bora Bora.

Special Interests

Bora Bora, French Polynesia

Shirley at Bora Bora

With my husband Tin Htoon

Special Interests

Bloody Mary Restaurant, Bora Bora

Boro Boro, French Polynesia

THE WORLD IS YOUR OYSTER

In Mauritius Red Sands

The Road Less Travelled

This phrase refers to places that are not often visited by many tourists. Some travelers desire to explore less-traveled countries. It also means daring to think differently and carve your own path.

I have a desire to travel not just for holidays, but for my work. In this book, I am sharing a lot of my experience since the publication of my first book in 1996/1997. Many people asked me to write two books - one on travel and another on my life experiences, balancing work, travel, family, and raising my two children. I declined the latter, thinking no one would be interested in my biography. However, in writing this travel book, I have included some of my life experiences. Thus, this book is unique as it combines my two intended books.

When I was studying for my Master of Science degree in Maternal and Child Health at the University of London in 1981, we were required to spend time in a country other than our own or the one we came from. My professor suggested I go to an organization in India where other students had gone the previous year. However, I wanted to carve my own path and do something different. So, I went to a less-visited place in West Bengal, 28 km from Calcutta, where I conducted my thesis research at the Child In Need Institute. The director had started a 6-month course for young girls to become MCH workers, covering 49 remote villages.

Before leaving London, my mentor and I printed out house numbers, but when I arrived in Dalautpur village, there were no house numbers or street names. I was having difficulty finding my way, especially since the director was out of the country. So, I followed the guidelines I learned in my London course, and started my research at the first house in a field where I threw a water bottle and let it point me in the direction of my first stop. This visit was a treasure, and I have written about other aspects of it in other chapters.

"Two roads diverged in a wood and I took the one less travelled by and that has made all the difference."

From Robert Frost's poem, *"The Road Not Taken,"* which is about how one choice can make a world of difference.

A few places less travelled:
    Tibet
    Mergui Archipelago
    The Silk Road

Chapter Four:
Different Modes of Transport

Travelling can be done in different ways, such as by car, cycling, train, airplane, or even by walking short distances. The mode of transportation chosen depends on several factors such as time, finances, different stages in life, work trips or holidays, and the age of the travellers.

People have different interests and can choose how they would like to travel, be it for work, holidays, individual or family trips, with friends, and for how many days and budget they have. It also depends on age, as young travellers may prefer physical activities like adventure tours, while older people may require a more comfortable and easy mode of travel.

From a young age up to now, I have travelled using all five modes of transport, including airplanes, train journeys, cruises, road trips by car and coaches, and even walking tours. If someone asked me which one I prefer, I would answer that I like them all, depending on what I am doing. For work, if I need to go to another country, I would travel by airplane as I would have to go quickly. I cannot go on a relaxing trip on a ship or train. For holidays, long or short, visiting friends, relatives, events, weddings, it all depends on how I will be travelling.

Air Travel

Air travel is a form of travel that includes vehicles such as airplanes, helicopters, hot air balloons, parachutes, and gliders.

Airplanes are the most common mode of air travel, offering fast service and the best advantage of airspeed, adopting the shortest route to reach the destination. They are excellent for travelling to far places or countries. The capacity of passengers on airplanes can vary, depending on whether it is a big or small plane, and which countries they travel to. The weight of the luggage in kilograms is also an important factor, as some airlines allow only one big baggage of 20-25kg in some parts of the world, while others allow up to two big suitcases or baggages for travel to the USA or European countries. In addition, passengers are allowed to take one small luggage on the plane, which can weigh up to 7kg. It is essential

Different Modes of Transport

to always check for baggage allowances and also what is permitted or not allowed on the plane.

Big airplanes have different classes, such as economy, premium economy, business class, first class, extra leg seat areas, and aisle seats. Some of the most famous airlines include United States Airlines, Singapore Airlines, New Zealand Airlines, Qatar Airways, Qantas Airline, Virgin Airlines, Japan Airlines, and Emirates.

For safety, the rear and middle seats are the most secure, while the aisle seats on either side in the middle of the aircraft are considered the worst seats in case of accidents or crashes. However, these seats are good for passengers who need to go to the toilet often on long flights. Window or middle seats in a three-seat arrangement can be difficult on long flights when the person next to you is sleeping and you need to get up. Some people like to walk to the back of the plane every two to three hours to prevent blood clots. For passengers with knee problems or leg and foot injuries, having more leg space on long flights is essential, and they may need to pay extra for this. Premium economy or business class fares can provide additional leg space.

Smaller airplanes do not fly very long flights. They fly to transit countries, where passengers switch to a bigger airplane to continue their journey. Smaller airplanes are used for domestic flights in countries like Australia, the United States, the United Kingdom, and Europe. They fly to different cities, and Mexican Airlines flies to various cities in Mexico. There are also many cheap airlines, such as Jetstar, Easy Jet, and Scoop, for short travels.

There are also small airplanes for about six people, as well as helicopters. It is great to fly with them and see places like the Great Barrier Reef from the air, the Grand Canyon, and the Himalayas. I have gone on these flights and seen the world from above. It is an amazing experience and very different from seeing things from the ground.

When travelling by air, I recommend that people who are unwell do not fly. During my many years of travel, I have encountered people who have become ill on flights. For example, I remember one lady who collapsed just after the seat belt signs were turned off. The plane was Singapore Airlines, and I was only in my early thirties, flying from Singapore to London, which would take about 13 hours. The pilot called for any doctor on board to help. I got up and saw a few flight attendants near one area, and I went there. The lady had fainted, but she was conscious when I saw her. I checked her temperature, blood pressure, heart sounds, and heart rate. Her blood pressure was slightly low, but her oxygen saturation was normal. She said she had been unwell for the past week, had not eaten or drunk much, and was very tired and fatigued. As I was checking her, another young male doctor came, and we both told the flight attendant to give her a cup of Milo or Ovaltine with sugar and milk and to let her lie down. We took her to a rear seat area where she could lie down.

Later, the pilot asked us whether the plane needed to land at the nearest place or continue flying. We told the pilot that it was not a heart attack and that the plane could continue flying. I checked on her every one to two hours during that flight. Most airlines have their ground-based physicians with whom they can ask for advice. The United States Airlines has an emergency consulting agency standing by to assist from the ground.

One incident occurred while I was travelling from Tokyo, Japan to Singapore. Shortly after the lunch meal, a passenger developed rashes on his arms and body, and quickly called for the flight attendant. A call was made for any doctor on board to help, and I responded. I checked the person's respiratory and chest sounds, and found them to be normal, with no wheezing. The person had allergies and was carrying an Epipen, which was also available on the plane. Instead of administering the Epipen, I gave the person one tablet of antihistamine (Telfast) and two tablets of Prednisolone 25mg, both of which were available in the plane's emergency kit. When I informed the crew that I was going to administer these medications, they asked to see my identity card and medical doctor card to ensure that I was trained to do so. Within 20 to 30 minutes of taking the medications, the person's rashes and itchiness slowly disappeared.

When I shared this experience with my medical colleagues upon my return to Singapore, they questioned why I didn't administer the Epipen. I explained that the person was not choking, had no wheezing or swelling of the eyes or mouth, and that I wanted to see how they responded to the antihistamine and steroid first. I was also concerned about the potential side effects of adrenaline (Epipen injection), such as increased heart rate and fast breathing, while we still had several hours left on the flight. Typically, if a doctor administers an Epipen for anaphylaxis, they would then call for an ambulance to take the person to the hospital.

In my 40 years of travel, I have responded to about 10 to 12 medical incidents, most of which were minor, such as children with ear pain or vomiting. The plane's emergency kit also includes Zofran wafer (Odansetron), which is used to treat nausea and vomiting. On larger planes, equipment for delivering babies during pregnancy is also available. Thankfully, I have never had to use this equipment.

Some of my friends have asked why I respond to medical emergencies when I am not covered by medical defense. While it is true that I am not covered by medical defense while on board a plane, I feel that it is my duty of care to help in any way I can to save lives. A study published in the New England Journal of Medicine found that there is typically one trained physician on board every 12 flights, and that medical emergencies are rare, occurring only once every 600 commercial flights.

There are certain medical conditions that make it unsafe for a person to fly, such as recent heart attacks or strokes, cardiac failure, epilepsy, recent surgeries, and contagious diseases. Additionally, pregnant women who are 36 weeks or more gestation are not allowed to travel by plane. When travelling long distances, it is advisable to take a stopover transit for one or two days in a country such as Singapore or Dubai to prevent fatigue and deep vein thrombosis (blood clots).

Some destinations cannot be reached by air travel alone. For example, after flying to Cairns, Australia, to see the Great Barrier Reef, visitors must take a ship or catamaran to reach the reef itself. Similarly, in Bora Bora, French Polynesia, after flying to Auckland, New Zealand, visitors typically spend a few days there before flying to Tahiti and then taking a boat to their resort on one of the many islands. In Venice, Italy, visitors must also take a boat to their hotel, as the city is built on canals. Despite these additional travel requirements, these destinations are well worth the extra effort.

Helicopter Trips or Small Planes?

Some people, such as my friends and colleagues in Singapore, are scared of traveling in small planes. However, when I was young and with my family in the USA, we flew with a pilot from Las Vegas to the Grand Canyon, and the view of the Grand Canyon from the plane was amazing.

Flying to the Grand Canyon

The World is Your Oyster

At the Grand Canyon USA

In Australia, my husband, daughter Kimberly, and I flew from Melbourne to Cairns in Queensland for a 10-day trip to the Great Barrier Reef. We traveled on a catamaran to visit the reef and went on a short submarine trip to see it up close. There was also an option for a one-hour helicopter or small plane ride to view the reef from above, but we decided not to go on the small plane. However, my husband regretted not going on the helicopter trip at Cairns.

After visiting the Great Barrier Reef, we flew down to Ali Beach on Hamilton Island. We went by boat and helicopter to see the Great Barrier Reef, which stretches from near Cairns down to Ali Beach and is one of the seven natural wonders of the world. We were lucky to have a beautiful and amazing helicopter trip from Hamilton Island, where we could see the little heart-shaped reef that couldn't be seen from the boat or ship. These types of plane trips provide us with the opportunity to see different sceneries and landscapes.

DIFFERENT MODES OF TRANSPORT

Flying from Hamilton Island Queensland to see Great Barrier Reef

From the plane we saw the Heart shape Barrier Reef, Amazing!

In Nepal 1990

Flying to see the Himalayas especially Mt Everest 1990

Different Modes of Transport

The view from the plane, the Himalayas including Mt Everest.

Isle of Wight Chairlifts in United Kingdom, When I was working in UK for a few months at Isle of Wight I went on the Chairlifts with a few friends

Railway Travel: Exploring the World by Train

Train journeys are a fantastic way to travel and I thoroughly enjoy them, even though some people find them boring. Travelling by rail can take you through scenic routes with breath-taking landscapes and sights that you may not see from a car or plane. Regardless of the distance, most countries have a train service, making it one of the most accessible modes of transportation.

One of the best things about travelling by train is that it is a relaxed way to arrive at the heart of your destination. You can take your time to admire the scenery, enjoy the comfort of your seat, and take in the different landscapes, including rivers, lakes, and wildlife.

Famous Train Journeys

The United Kingdom has a vast rail network that covers the entire country, with trains travelling from London to Birmingham, Manchester, Scotland, Southend-on-Sea, and Cardiff in Wales. The London Underground also connects to the Eurostar, which travels to Paris and the rest of Europe.

Rail journeys winding around the Swiss Alps are also incredibly popular, and Spain boasts modern rail journeys, including the luxurious Orient Express.

Another well-known train journey is the Qinghai-Tibet Railway, which connects Xining in Qinghai province to Lhasa, making it the world's highest train journey. The Tanggula station, situated 4m lower, is the highest railway station globally.

Lastly, African Rail Journeys offers the Blue Train, which takes you through the scenic landscapes of South Africa.

My Amazing Train Journeys

Japan:
The first high-speed rail system began operations in Japan in 1964 and is known as the Shinkansen or the "bullet train". Japan now has nine high-speed rail lines serving 22 of its major cities stretching across its three main islands, and they are still developing more rail lines.

I have been to Japan a few times, for work and family holidays. I visited Mt. Fuji a few times, but the best view I saw was while I was travelling on the Shinkansen train. The view was amazing, just like the pictures we see on calendars with one mountain covered in snow. The Shinkansen was started in 1964, and over the years, they changed the speed per hour and improved the technology. The latest Shinkansen is the Shinkansen 700S (700 Supreme), which started before the Tokyo Olympics in 2020. When they developed different Shinkansen trains, the manager said on a TV program that with technology, it is made for more safety, as Japan gets earthquakes, and the winter season is very cold with a lot of snow.

Shinkansen train and the view of Mt Fuji is extremely beautiful.

The Ghan train in Australia:
My daughter and I went on this rail journey. We flew from Melbourne to Adelaide, Southern Australia. The Ghan train starts from Adelaide to Darwin, Northern Territory, Australia, for three days and two nights. It stops at Katherine and Alice Springs.

It was a very beautiful and amazing trip. The landscapes were beautiful, with the red sand desert and salt lake. The Ghan is regarded as a legendary train and one of the world's greatest rail journeys. On that train, big luggage cannot be put in cabins as the cabins are small. We were going on a long holiday, so after we arrived in Darwin, we stayed for five days, and then we flew to Uluru and stayed there for another five days. We had a big luggage, so we had to take out some clothes for the three days that we would use on the train. They gave us a bag, and the suitcase was put in the train's luggage compartment. There is a luxury cabin that is more spacious. All the cabins have a table and a bathroom where you can shower and use the toilet in your room.

THE WORLD IS YOUR OYSTER

Only breakfast, lunch, and dinner were in one area of the train. There is a big area where people on the train can sit and chat with one another, and there is a café that has all drinks, coffee, tea, or cold drinks, and a lot of snacks. These can be taken anytime, and the staff are there. On the way, they stop at Katherine and Alice Springs, and people are given tours for a few hours to see the place. My daughter went on one tour, and I went to The Flying Doctors in the Central part of Australia, where any emergencies needed to be addressed. It is difficult to go to hospitals or travel, so you can call them, and the reception will quickly arrange a plane, a pilot, a doctor, and a nurse. They will quickly do any possible emergency treatment and take the person to the nearest hospital. There is a short video of how the Flying Doctors in Red Central was started and how they save lives. It was very good and interesting. I was glad that I managed to know and learn about the Flying Doctors and have been to their original location.

The whole journey was amazing! I cannot understand why some people think train journeys are boring. We saw beautiful landscapes, sceneries, and different kinds of trees. We saw beautiful sunset views, wild camels, and wild horses roaming around. The Ghan Rail journey should be on the bucket list of many travelers.

The Ghan Train

Different Modes of Transport

Shirley and Kimberly went on the Ghan Railway Journey from Adelaide, South Australia to Darwin Northern Territory Australia, 3 days 2 nights journey. Amazing!

Europe Rail Journey:
Another rail journey that I went on with my daughter was a Europe rail trip.

We traveled to five to six countries and 13 cities in Europe with the Eurail Pass. My daughter, who had just finished Year 12, was only 17 years old and this was her first visit to Europe. She planned the entire trip, booking tickets and hotels, and was clever in choosing hotels close to railway stations. We planned to stay for about six to eight weeks.

We flew from Melbourne to London, spent five days there, then took the Eurostar train to Paris. From there, we visited another city in France every four to five days, then traveled to Italy, Monaco, and Spain. We added Spain to our itinerary as I had not visited it when I was younger.

We spent most of our time in Barcelona, with two days in Madrid and one day in Seville. We purchased the Eurail Pass to travel within Europe by rail. However, when we tried to take the overnight train from Venice to Barcelona, it was completely booked, so we flew with Easy Jet instead.

After about five to six weeks, we still had one or two countries left on our Eurail Pass, but we decided to skip them and fly back to Singapore. We stayed there for eight days before flying back to Australia. Some of my friends were surprised by our trip, asking, "What age do you think you are?" because I was not young and was traveling like someone 18 to 20 years old, exploring many countries, cities, and walking long distances with luggage. Despite being a bit tiring, we thoroughly enjoyed the experience.

During our travels, we also went on a six-hour train journey from Oslo to Bergen in Norway, which was very beautiful, with amazing waterfalls, fjords, and landscapes. I also took a train journey along the River Rhine in Germany, which lasted several hours. I enjoyed looking out at the river, which was very beautiful. We also traveled on overnight and day trip trains, sometimes for six to seven hours or longer.

In China, we spent three to four days visiting the Terracotta Warriors after traveling on an overnight train from Beijing to Xi'an. In India, we took overnight trains, and in Burma, we traveled from Rangoon to Mandalay on a 12-hour train journey from 6 am to 6 pm.

We also took the Eurostar train from London to Paris and traveled by rail to many other cities in the UK. Finally, we took a train journey from Helsinki, Finland, to St. Petersburg, Russia.

Road Trips

Road trips, whether by car, coach, or caravan, are a great way to travel and explore. They offer a flexible and customizable itinerary, making them a popular choice for short holidays or one-two-week trips with family, friends, or partners. One advantage of road trips is that you can start your journey in the morning and take breaks whenever you need them.

Different Modes of Transport

When traveling on a coach group tour, you are often given a specific departure time and itinerary. Hotels may even provide breakfast packs for these tours. You can choose to go on short or long trips, depending on how many weeks you are traveling.

Coach tour UK

With Kimberly in London, United Kingdom

Coach Tour, in USA

Different Modes of Transport

In Beijing, China

With son Shai Wan and daughter Kimberly in China

The World is Your Oyster

In my introduction, I wrote about my amazing road trip in Burma. I have also been on road trips in other countries. In 1979, while in the UK, I went on a coach tour to France, Paris, and Versailles for two weeks. In Canada and the USA, I went on coach tours to different cities and even on a Rocky Mountain Tour. In Australia, I went on coach tours to snow places like Mt. Buller.

Traveling by your own car allows you to stop when you need to rest or eat, and you can choose when and where to stop. However, it can be tiring to drive for long periods of time. If traveling with friends or family, you can take turns driving.

One amazing road trip I had was in 1980 during Easter holiday while studying for my MSc Maternal and Child Health course in London. A friend of mine, who was also studying the same course and had a car, drove us and two other students to Amsterdam. We had lunch at a restaurant in Belgium, saw beautiful scenery, and visited places where they make lace . We stayed in a house for a week with four other students from our course in Amsterdam and rented a van to travel together .We saw many Windmills, and tulips gardens. We return back the Road trip. It was an unforgettable trip.

When we came to Australia, we lived in Victoria's Mornington Peninsula, one of the most beautiful places in Australia. I drove from Mt. Eliza to Sorrento with my youngest sister, Rosie, and my daughter, Kimberly, when she was only about 11 years old. At Sorrento, we parked the car and went on the ship that goes to Queenscliff in Portsea. Our friends came to pick us up, took us to their home, and also drove us around the other side of the Peninsula. We returned by the ship again and drove back to our home.

On another trip to the other side of the Peninsula with my husband, we drove and then put the car on the ship. The ship went to Port Sea for about an hour and arrived at Queenscliff, and we drove to the picnic spot our friends arranged. Later, we drove back from that side of the Peninsula to Melbourne city and then drove back to Mornington Peninsula. We did not need to go back on the ship again. The trips can be different, depending on where you are going and when you have time to spare, for relaxing trips.

We went by car from Victoria Melbourne to Canberra many times as we go for Embassy functions. Going on self-road trips is good; you can travel and stop where you like, which is different from coaches, where you are together with other people.

From my several road trips in London and Australia, I have come across other cars having traffic accidents. Once in Australia, a truck fell, and the driver was not injured, but the truck was lying on the two small lanes, and the road was completely blocked. We had to wait for over an hour until that truck was cleared. In the UK, two road trips to Oxford, which took two hours, took nearly three hours as there was a road accident, and the cars couldn't move. Also, coming back from Oxford, there was an accident in front again.

Different Modes of Transport

When you are going for work, interview, or meeting, you always need to go a bit early for those. For a holiday, there is no fixed time, so it is okay.

Caravan Trips

Some people own a caravan, and a luxurious caravan has beds, toilets, fridge, cooker, and they can travel the whole country. They stop over at caravan parks. Some people rent a caravan and travel for a holiday. I think retirees, when they have time to relax, it would be good to travel in caravans, and they can stop when they want at caravan parking places. If tired, they can sleep in their caravan; there is no need to go to hotels or motels. Big countries like Australia, USA, and Canada caravan trips will be good.

Cycling Tours

Cycling tours are also road trips. I did some cycling when I was young, only short ones near our home, not tours or trips. I have met a few people who have done cycling tours. A doctor with whom I worked in Australia went with a group of cyclist friends for a week trip cycling in Regional Victoria. Another was a patient in my clinic; he said he went on cycling tours for six months in Europe, covering many countries. In Switzerland, cycling mountaineering along the Alps are tourist highlights.

Walking Tours

Walking tours are also a part of road trips. You can walk and visit places, scenic beauty, or famous tourist spots. Walking tours are also very good with travel tour guides in historical places, museums, or cathedrals. I am writing to give some advice. Many people think that they can go on these walking tours by themselves and do not need a tour guide. However, if you are traveling to a place for the first time, the tour guide will explain all the history, the buildings, and what was done in those areas.

We have traveled a few times ourselves to some very famous or popular areas, thinking that when we see them, we will know everything. It is not the same as having a tour guide explain everything to you. Sometimes, I have read about the country, city, or place before I travel.

Walking tours can be part of coach tours, where people go on the coach and get down at different places to do a walking tour with their guide. They can also be part of train journeys or cruise tours. When the train stops, people can go on a walking tour for a few hours, and when the cruise ship stops at a port, people can go on a car ride or a walking tour in the morning after breakfast.

When I traveled with my daughter on the Ghan train journey in Australia, and when the train stopped at Alice Springs, I went on a walking tour to the Flying Doctors Center, and Kimberly went on another walking tour. We could choose different ones we liked to see and visit.

Only when getting older and having knee or foot problems, walking and climbing some steps become difficult. I had many walking tours during my travels, many in Europe, in China during the Yangtze River cruise, and also in Norway. They were all very beautiful, and the tour guides explained a lot about history.

In some places, you cannot go by car or other methods. You have to walk or climb, like in Dubrovnik, Croatia, where the landscape is such that you can only go on foot.

For many walking tours, a coach will come and pick you up at your hotel and then drop off all the people who are visiting that place nearby. From that spot, you can go walking and stop at different places, and the tour guide will explain the place, the building, and the scenery. It is very good if the place has history, spectacular beauty, and you have to do some climbing.

Cruises, Ship, and Boat Tours - QE2 Cruise Ship

I went on the famous QE2 Cruise Ship in March 2008 with my mum and daughter. We started our journey from Sydney and traveled to nearly all states of Australia before sailing to Singapore. This QE2 Cruise was one of my dream destinations.

The trip was very relaxing and enjoyable thanks to the helpful and respectful captain and staff members. The ship started from Sydney Harbour and traveled down to Bass Strait, Hobart, Tasmania, Melbourne, Albany, Adelaide, and Perth. At every state of Australia where the ship stopped in the evening, we would get off the ship after breakfast the next morning and go on the tours we selected.

My mum didn't visit all states, only Melbourne, as we live there. She would leave the ship to shower, eat lunch at a restaurant, and bring new clothes back to the ship. My mum went out of the ship at Perth to visit our close family friends who fetched us, took us to their home, had lunch, and showed us two tourist spots. One of which was the famous Park, more beautiful in Spring.

On the ship, after dinner and just after the main meal, a birthday cake with candles was brought to our table, and the birthday song played. It was Kimberly's birthday, and it was a surprise as we weren't planning on celebrating.

The ship has cafes, restaurants, theaters, movies, swimming pools, gyms, dancing lessons, and more. After the first day, we came aboard, and the next day was a welcome party where the captain, medical doctors, staff, nurses, and others joined, and we got to know them. It was good that we knew them so that we could get help if anything went wrong.

Different Modes of Transport

QE2 Cruise Ship World Famous

After the ship finished going to those states, it sailed to Singapore for about three days, and we were on the ship all the time. Some people think cruises are boring as you are on the ship, but it is not all the time. We visited five states in Australia and visited each day in that state. After that, I went around the ship, but I don't think I went to all places on the ship. The ship has many levels, and on these luxury cruise ships, there is a floor where they sell like a shopping complex. I went there and bought many things which you never see in normal stores in the cities or in the country. It was amazing, and I bought things to give as presents. I was happy that I managed to go on my dream destination cruise ship.

THE WORLD IS YOUR OYSTER

On Queen Elizabeth 2 ship at Hobart, Tasmania, Australia

Another Queen Elizabeth Cruise Ship - New Cunard One for Two to Three Weeks

I went on this trip with my husband. We flew to Singapore first and stayed there for three days before going on the ship. The ship sailed to Sri Lanka, and we went to one place ourselves with a taxi. We ate at a famous seaside restaurant at a hotel and then came back to the ship. We didn't go on a tour as we had been to Sri Lanka a few years ago and gone on tours for about eight days. We saw Lord Buddha's sacred temple of Tooth in Kandy, where there is a Bodhi tree. The daughter of King Ashoka, Arahath Sanghamitra, brought a sapling of the Bodhi tree in Buddha Gaya to Sri Lanka. The Sapling of the Bodhi tree, known as Jaya Sri Maha Bodhi, was planted in the Mahameghavana Park in Anuradhapura by the King Devanampiya Tisa.

After stopping at Sri Lanka, the ship sailed that night to Seychelles. After stopping in Seychelles, we went on a day tour and saw the big Tortoises in parks, and a few tourist spots.

After visiting Seychelles, the ship sailed to Mauritius where we went on a day tour. The place was very beautiful, Red sands . From there, we sailed to South Africa and stopped for a day before heading to Cape Town. Although the ship stopped in Cape Town for two days, we decided to get down as we planned to stay there for 5 to 6 days. During our stay, we visited many places such as the Nelson Mandela prison and also took a tour drive along the sea and Table Mountain, which were all so beautiful that we even thought about living there.

DIFFERENT MODES OF TRANSPORT

Another new Cunard Queen Elizabeth Ship

After leaving South Africa, we flew to Zambia and visited Zambia and Zimbabwe for about eight days. One of my dream destinations was Victoria Falls, and even when the person booking our travel suggested visiting only one country to see the falls, I still wanted to see them from both countries. We went on the bridge with a car two times and once walking, stood there, and took pictures. It was an amazing trip.

For the Hurtigruten cruise ship trip in Norway, I flew from Melbourne to Oslo, where my daughter Kimberly joined me after doing a few months of placement in neuro-science in Singapore. From Oslo, we went on a six-hour train journey to Bergen, and the scenery was amazing with waterfalls and fjords. We stayed in Bergen for a few days before going on the Hurtigruten ship. This trip was one of my best trips, and my daughter has even written about it together in her chapter.

From Hurtigruten Cruise ship which ever city it stops we go with their coach tour

Different Modes of Transport

In Norway 2016

Norway, Arctic Mother and Daughter, 8th Feb 2016

THE WORLD IS YOUR OYSTER

During our visit to China in 2016, my son Shai Wan, Kimberly, and I flew to Beijing and spent about five days visiting Tiananmen Square, the Great Wall, and watching shows. We then took a train journey to Xi An, where we saw the Terracotta Warriors and then went on the Yangtze River Cruise for about eight days. The Yangtze River is the world's third-longest river, the longest in Eurasia, and the longest in the world to flow entirely within one country, flowing through the whole country of China, covering 6,300 km. It was an amazing trip, with stops at different cities and beautiful views of caves and fjords. The 3 Gorges Dam on the Yangtze river is the largest hydro-power station in the world.

On Yantze River Cruise, China with son Shai Wan and daughter Kimberly

DIFFERENT MODES OF TRANSPORT

Yantze River Cruise, China

Mekong River Cruise, Laos

I have also gone on Mekong River cruises in Laos and Vietnam. The Mekong River is the 12th longest river in the world and the third longest in Asia, covering 4,909 km. It flows through six countries: China, Burma, Thailand, Laos, Cambodia, and Vietnam. I have been to the Golden Triangle in Southeast Asia, where the borders of Thailand, Laos, and Myanmar meet at the confluence of the Ruak and Mekong Rivers.

Lastly, during my visit to Zambia and Zimbabwe, I went on the Zambezi River cruise, which was a lovely and beautiful trip. The Zambezi River flows through Zambia, Zimbabwe, and one can also see Namibia and Botswana.

Danube River Cruise

The Danube River begins in Germany's Black Forest and flows through many countries, including Austria, Slovakia, Hungary, Croatia, Serbia, Bulgaria, Romania, Moldova, and Ukraine before it reaches the Black Sea. Although I've been to many of these countries, I didn't see the Danube in Germany or Austria. In Croatia, I also missed seeing the river, but in Serbia, I saw both the Danube and Sava rivers in Belgrade, where the two rivers converge. The city's Belgrade Fortress and Kalemegdan Park offer fantastic views of the two rivers. When I visited Budapest, Hungary, I took a Danube River cruise and saw the river flowing on one side of Buda and the other side of Pest, with views of the Parliament building.

On Danube Cruise in Budapest, Hungary

Different Modes of Transport

As a child, I played piano and loved the Blue Danube Waltz by Johann Strauss. Seeing the Danube River was a dream come true for me. I also saw André Rieu's concert in Melbourne where he played the Beautiful Blue Danube Waltz.

River Thames

I saw the River Thames in Oxford and mostly in London, where I lived for two years while studying for my Master of Science in Maternal and Child Health. I went on a Thames River cruise a few times, either by myself or with friends.

River Ganges

When I visited India in 1981, I spent two months traveling around New Delhi, Agra, Jaipur, and Varanasi, where I saw the River Ganges. In 2015, I took a boat ride on the river with my husband.

River Ganges boat ride with my husband in India 2015

Irrawaddy River Cruise

The Irrawaddy River flows throughout Burma, and I've been on the river twice while traveling with 100 outstanding students. I wrote about this experience in my introduction chapter.

Chapter Five:
An Interlude

Kimberly's Experience in Travelling
(Child and Young Adult's Perspective)

My parents have always loved to travel, and unsurprisingly, they have also cultivated this desire to explore the world in my brother and myself, too. We were lucky enough to be whisked away to Disneyland and the Grand Canyon as children, as we have relatives in the US, and living in Singapore meant very easy visits to many Asian countries such as Myanmar (part of our roots), Thailand, and Malaysia. Because of this, I never considered travelling a luxury, I just thought it was the norm.

My family and I in Myanmar. approximately 1996.

An Interlude

However, moving to Australia made me realise that I am incredibly fortunate to have such experiences and memories, as there are many people out there who have never left their home country and have never had the opportunity to. If I had to take away only one life lesson from my parents, it is to always be grateful for what I have and to appreciate everything around me. What I love most about travelling is learning and immersing yourself in the culture of another country, seeing things you normally would not see in your own neighbourhood and appreciating someone else's way of life. Without travelling, I believe it would be impossible to have an open mind. Travelling opens your eyes and widens your horizons in ways you do not expect, and you always return home slightly altered.

When my mother asked me to be a small part of her book, I said yes. I wanted to make her proud, and create something with her that we would both cherish in the future. She is the reason why I have a love for travel in the first place, and it is the least I can do for someone who has always been there for me. However, as I began to write it, I found it quite difficult to put my jumbled-up thoughts into eloquent paragraphs, into sentences that people would want to read, and I had no idea what points and take-away messages I actually wanted to convey to the reader.

After giving it some thought, I would like my chapter to discuss:
1. What it is like growing up with parents who enjoy travelling
2. How to transition from someone who travels with people to someone who travels alone
3. How it differs travelling with family versus travelling with a partner, or some friends
4. Some particularly memorable trips I've had in recent times

I do not remember much of our family trips as a child, and I only began remembering the holidays we have had probably after the age of ten or so, especially once we moved to Melbourne, Australia and it was just my mother and I on holiday together. As it was just the two of us in Australia for about five or so years, with the occasional visit from my brother and father (my brother was in the army at the time, while my father was still working in Singapore and unable to move with us), the holidays we took together became more memorable. My mother has always been someone who works hard in her career, but is also constantly planning a holiday somewhere. Her favourite place to go to in our little neighbourhood was the travel agency, to discuss potential holiday destinations.

Perhaps, she is the reason why I am always seeking out the next exciting destination too, and why I strive for a work-life balance where I am happy and successful in my career, but also still able to enjoy life and enjoy the time I have right now by exploring other parts of the world. My father also enjoys travelling, and when he was younger, he travelled in a different way. In his twenties, he became a seaman and had the chance to travel to exciting places such as Egypt, way back in the 1970s. Now, he enjoys the comfort of being at home and tending to his garden, but in their retirement years, my parents have enjoyed trips to South Africa, Bora Bora, etc. You can say that they worked hard to be able to play hard now, and enjoy their time together again. It always amazes me how my father came from humble beginnings, and became successful enough to give us this wonderful, comfortable life, allowing these opportunities to travel, something that I will always cherish.

Me with my mother and father in Siem Reap. Cambodia. 2009.

Naturally, if you started off travelling with family, as you get older, you begin to want to explore the world for yourself, on your own terms. My first experience of travelling without my family was during a high school camp to the USA when I was 15, where we had teachers looking after us and I was with 20 or so other girls. I would not say that it eased me into travelling without family, but it definitely showed me that I do not get homesick easily, which is a lesson in itself. It also allowed me to learn how to respect other people around me that are not family, and I felt that I also learned how to read people better, too. In one example, it

An Interlude

was the first time my closest friend on the trip was away from her parents, too, and she felt homesick once or twice during the trip. On those days, she seemed to withdraw and become quieter, which I took as my cue that she wanted space and time to herself, so I left her to her own devices. When she was ready, she started engaging more again and that's how I knew that she was okay. That trip felt like the first taste of 'freedom' in a way, because I was travelling with people my age and my parents were not around to watch my every move, but we were still restricted as it was a school trip.

After that, I became more comfortable with taking planes on my own and not needing someone by my side to keep me company or look after me. Now, having moved to the UK alone, and being in a long-distance relationship where my partner and I would try and meet in various places, it has become second nature to me. Here are some tips on how to make travelling alone fun and bearable:

1. Pack lightly, and pack something you're sure you can carry yourself, especially if you are bringing cabin baggage (personally, I am very short so I always check in my luggage).
2. Kindles/e-readers are great for travelling—all your books on one device and you can get sucked into a book for hours on a flight.
3. Take an aisle seat if it's available, so that the bathroom is always accessible, unless you are someone who doesn't move once they are comfortable on a plane (me on long-haul flights), then choose a window seat so that people who like getting up (my mother) have the chance to.
4. If the person next to you looks approachable, why not strike up a conversation? My mother is particularly good at this, and is able to chat with anyone, it is surprisingly refreshing, as I tend to keep to myself. However, if I find someone fun to talk to, it really does make a flight much more enjoyable.
5. If you get motion sickness on a plane, I find sleeping throughout the flight very helpful and it is definitely worth investing in a travel pillow and an eye mask.
6. Get a powerful portable power bank charger (Anker is a good brand) so that none of your devices run out of battery!

What I find important, in the lead up to a solo flight, is to make a checklist of all the things you want in your backpack or cabin bag, and to think about what you actually want to do and achieve during the flight. I think this helps you narrow down the essentials, so you don't end up bringing heavy and useless items. Also, I can be quite forgetful, so having a checklist ensures I know what is in my bag, and can do a final check before I leave the plane.

I know the idea of travelling alone can be daunting to people, and I still get anxious sometimes when I know it is coming up, but once you're in the process of going to the airport, checking in your luggage, etc. I think your brain goes into autopilot mode, and responsibility kicks in, and that sense of anxiety disappears because you know that you need to go through the motions. I also like to think of the potential duty-free shopping I might do to get myself excited about going through airports alone. Another tip, if you are transiting through a big airport, it doesn't hurt to look at a map of the place first, so you familiarise yourself with the layout. I did this with Istanbul Airport, when it first became the big commercial airport in April 2019 (our flights were in May 2019) and it really helped just knowing how far I might have to walk to my next gate. Lastly, if you are someone who lives far away from the airport you are travelling from, and sometimes feel anxious about the journey to the airport on the day of your flight, I find that staying in a cheap hotel the night before really helps ease my anxiety, as I know that I'm close to the airport and should not run into any problems where I might miss my flight. If it takes me longer than usual the night before to get to the hotel, it's okay as my flight is not scheduled until the next day. I hope these tips are helpful, and soon enough you'll be handling solo plane trips like a pro!

Now, I would like to discuss the differences between travelling with family, friends and a significant other. I have been lucky enough to have experience in travelling with various counterparts, starting naturally with family. When I travelled with my family, I was younger and dependent on my parents, and so everything was planned out for me and my brother, as we would just follow the itinerary that my parents created. Nothing wrong with that, as my parents always chose to go to the most popular landmarks, allowing me to see the country and what it offered. Now, as I'm older and have developed my own interests, I look back at some of my family holidays and regret not eating more, not smiling more in pictures, etc. I find that while I overall enjoyed my time with family, and the exotic places my mother would organise trips to, they are definitely not as memorable as the ones that I have planned myself. For example, we had a great trip to Japan during cherry blossom season back in 2009, but I look back at the photos and as a self-proclaimed foodie, regret not exploring the food scene more, as Japan is so well known for their cuisine. I suppose now, it gives me all the more reason to go back, which isn't a bad thing at all. Additionally, as my parents get older, they are no longer able to be as active as they used to be, and so moving, walking, and exploring becomes much harder, so countries that are not as well-developed, or countries with a lot of adventure activities as highlights are no longer possible to do. My mother always says that she wishes she went to certain countries when she was younger as they are too difficult to do now. I think of family holidays as comfortable and relaxing, less so adventurous and more so quality time spent together. Most importantly, cherish the times you are able to travel as a family. Looking back now, and looking at family holiday photos together, being able to travel with both my parents and my brother has become such a rarity, and I wish we did it more before my brother and I moved to different parts of the world.

An Interlude

My family and myself in Thailand. approximately 1997.

Meanwhile, travelling with friends is much more involved. At my age, early-to-mid-twenties, we are young, living our best lives and frankly, mostly broke. We are either dependent on our parents for money, or we have just started out work-wise, so we have not had the time to gather some savings. That's okay, we're not the only ones in this boat, but it does mean travelling is nowhere near as extravagant as a family trip. The few trips I've had with friends have involved thorough research on what hotel we should stay at, how much it is and what budget we have to stick to. I remember in particular, when my friend and I were planning a trip to New York City—finding accommodation was SO difficult as it is such an expensive city, and we looked for days and weeks and were constantly throwing options at each other, and as we were about to book, the price would have gone up due to popularity, and it was overall a little bit of a nightmare. We ended up finding somewhere that was probably three stars at best, but figured that we would only ever be back in our hotel room to sleep. We focused on location, rather than five-star facilities, and that is how I've always looked for hotels since. I do not need luxury facilities for the week-long trip, I just want a bed and a five-minute walk to a metro station, please.

Next to the Statue of Liberty. New York City. 2016.

An Interlude

I personally really enjoy travelling with friends, as I love planning trips. I love researching the best deals for exploring a city, the sales for tourist landmark tickets, if a student card qualifies as concession status, and what time all the famous landmarks close, so we can plan an itinerary accordingly, and figure out how many places we can see in a day while we're in the area. I love looking up the best food places and figuring out how to get there for lunch, and looking up what to eat for dinner that's around the hotel. I find that by being so involved with the planning and the research, the trip becomes much more exciting and you have more to look forward to, and you really get your money's worth when you find amazing deals. I think travelling with the right kind of people really does enhance your experience, and so far I've been lucky to have only had positive trips with different friends. It really helps when you're both easygoing and flexible, and open-minded to whatever the other person suggests. I always find that the excitement of being in a new city or country relaxes everyone and the trip becomes more enjoyable. Less so with family, and more with friends, you need to learn to read the room more, and you need to be more careful about how you act, as you will never be as comfortable with them as you would your own family. However, that doesn't mean it's a bad thing; I think it helps you become more aware of your surroundings. I think also it helps with being more frugal financially, because neither of you want to spend all your money within the first few days of a trip, so you keep each other accountable. You develop a sense of responsibility that you would not if you were travelling with family, who would be able to pay for whatever you need. When travelling with friends, I'd recommend bringing practical shoes so your feet don't hurt, because almost every time I travel with friends, I've found myself inadvertently walking thousands of steps without thinking, and as someone who generally wears terrible shoes (flats with no support), it is not fun for anyone when you're bleeding from blisters and need new shoes as soon as possible. Dress comfortably! Also, I like to bring an empty bag for shopping, because chances are, you and your friend both like to shop and will end up shopping together, so it's a safe space to spend whatever extra money you have at the end of the trip.

Lastly, in the past few years of my life, I've been so thankful and grateful to have the most supportive and loving partner by my side. He has supported me while I moved from Australia to the United Kingdom, and he continues to support me daily, just by being around. Luckily, he loves travelling, too, and probably has way more experience in this regard than I do. He grew up with a family that constantly moved countries because of work, and because of this, has experienced many more cultures than I have. He is very open-minded but grounded, and our relationship has continued to allow both of us to nurture this love for travelling, as the long distance has allowed us to meet in interesting places, and travel to new countries together. While we have each seen part of the world on our own, we are now trying to see the rest of the world together. So far, we have travelled to Turkey, Ireland, Taiwan, Cuba, and Vietnam together, and are hoping to travel around Europe more in the future now that we have both settled in the UK for a while. I was quite unsure at first about travelling with a significant other, as dating someone and being around them 24 hours, 7 days a week, are completely different experiences, but we surprisingly fell into it quite comfortably. It definitely helps that we are both very easygoing, and if I want to plan something or go to specific food places, he is always fine with it. I like to plan more than he does, so I try to keep things flexible, where I say I want to go to certain places, and we try and fit it around the time that we have, and he tends to mention experiences that he wants to do, go on a food tour in a country, or visit a whisky distillery since he likes whisky. When I travel with him, I try not to make things too rigid as it can get overwhelming, and travelling together is all about compromise. I think travelling with a partner is all about making sure we each get the most out of a country, so making sure we both leave with no regrets is key, and I always make sure to not steamroll my way through to get everything I want, but nothing that he wants, as that is unfair and makes for only a fun trip for one. Be warned: little fights are inevitable, and almost healthy when you are travelling together. No matter how easygoing you both are, you will still have disagreements over how much to spend and what to do, that's natural. Don't worry about it if that happens, it will be resolved soon enough and you'll continue to have a great time. I believe travelling together is an important rite of passage in a relationship as you learn a lot about your partner that you may not necessarily notice during day-to-day life and it really helps a person realise if they are truly compatible with their significant other or not. I will delve into this more when I talk about one of my more memorable trips.

My partner Nihal and myself in Havana. Cuba. 2019.

An Interlude

Now, moving on to the final part of my chapter, I thought it would be nice to discuss a few of my favourite trips in recent times, and what made them so special.

Norway/Finland/Russia 2016

In the Australian summer of 2015/2016, I had just finished a two-and-a-half-month internship in a lab in Singapore and I was ready for a holiday. It was rather last minute and I remember being in Singapore the week before leaving and shopping frantically for appropriate clothes for the cold winter because all I had in my suitcase was summer attire. Needless to say, I was not prepared. I was very excited, because it had been years since I had been to Europe, and Norway, Finland and Russia were completely new countries to both my mother and myself. Luckily, it completely exceeded my expectations. It was unexpected, it took us to completely unique places and we saw and experienced things that we otherwise would not have seen, such as dog-sledding and the Northern Lights.

Norway is truly beautiful, especially Bergen, this beautiful little town that the cruise we took started in. It was so peaceful and people were so friendly and it has completely stolen my heart. We spent about three nights there prior to the start of our cruise, and honestly I wish we had longer. The weather was perfect for roaming around, and we found the tourist service centre to be convenient and friendly. I would say my favourite part of Bergen was simply just walking down the streets and appreciating how different everything was to Singapore and Australia. How comfortable and safe it felt to walk down these streets even though the place was completely foreign to us, and how happy and relaxed everyone seemed. Bergen had a 45- minute to one-hour-long cable car ride that took you to the top of Bergen, and the views were breathtaking!

THE WORLD IS YOUR OYSTER

At the top of Bergen, Norway, 2016.

Besides the few days we had in Bergen, we spent most of our time in Norway on a cruise specifically designed for people to see the Northern Lights, a company called Hurtigruten Cruises. The cruise is like any other cruise, where you have a small, but expensive room that you only use for sleeping but what I enjoyed most about the cruise were the constant stream of activities they had available to you (if you pay extra), at the various ports. We had a stop at Trondheim, and we did a Trondheim City Walk which was lovely, with a guide who showed us various important landmarks of the town, we went to the North Cape, the northernmost point in Norway, I nearly got to drive a snowmobile, but sadly it got cancelled because conditions were not ideal, and what was possibly my favourite activity of the entire holiday, we had the chance to go dog-sledding in Tromso, that even my mother joined in on. Even now, looking back on it years later, that still feels like such a once-in-a-lifetime experience, and somehow, having done it in the Arctic Circle makes it all the more special.

An Interlude

Dog-sledding with my mum, Tromso, Norway, 2016.

Additionally, this cruise is the reason why we even got to see the Northern Lights in the first place! They even have a Northern Lights promise stated on their website, where if you do not see the Northern Lights on your voyage, they will give you another 6–7-day voyage free of charge. We were lucky to see it on the cruise the first time, so we didn't have to trek all the way back to Norway from Australia again. I remember the moment distinctly. We had just left our cabin for dinner, and we had finished our starters and were onto our mains, when the captain of the boat casually announced that the Northern Lights were on display over the PA. There was a moment of stunned silence amongst the crowd, and then suddenly everyone dropped their cutlery onto their plates and started rushing back to their cabins to grab their cameras and coats because it was freezing outside before heading out to the upstairs deck. I remember wearing shoes that were not at all appropriate for the deck, and kept almost slipping because it was so wet outside, but the view was mesmerising. My mum and I stood outside for a while, frantically trying to get one decent shot of the Northern Lights and also just enjoying these flickering green lights before our very eyes. I think we stood outside for an hour or two, bravely facing the cold, harsh wind because we could not believe we actually got to see it. Every once in a while, I think back on that night and how lucky my mother and I were to have that experience together. The only thing I regret is not having better photography equipment to catch the moment with. I remember doing extensive research as to what I had to do to get some photos of the Northern Lights, so we purchased a tripod and brought our DSLR Nikon D90 with us on the trip, and while the photos are amateur-level at best, we were just relieved to have photos to remember the time by.

Northern Lights, seen near Tromso, Norway, 2016.

An Interlude

After we had accomplished our bucket list goal, the rest of the trip seemed like a bonus, and we still had Helsinki and Saint Petersburg to do. In Helsinki, we were only there for a night and it rained the entire time, so we spent the day doing some much needed retail therapy. To this day, my favourite earrings that I wear almost every day are from Helsinki, and I haven't seen a pair like them since. It was also my mother's birthday in Helsinki, and so we treated ourselves to a nice meal and enjoyed a relaxing day, which was much needed after being cooped up on a cruise for the past week or so.

Saint Petersburg was a complete surprise. I had no idea what to expect, and my mother had organised it with the travel agency as it was close to Helsinki and it was a new country to add to my mother's list, but it blew me away. The architecture was stunning, in particular the Church of the Savior on Spilled Blood, the Winter Palace, now the State Hermitage Museum and the Catherine Palace. The Hermitage Museum is an absolute must-go just to see all the rooms on the inside and how it was decorated in such a lavish fashion. It is so big that it warrants multiple visits if you have the time, as you definitely will not cover everything in one visit. My experience of Saint Petersburg helped me realise that sometimes it's good to dive into the unknown and not do too much research on a place, as it can completely throw you off guard (usually in a good way). I think the fact that I had no idea what to expect made the place much more memorable, and I cannot wait to go back one day. For Saint Petersburg, I would recommend getting a hotel in the heart of the city so that you can walk to all the landmarks, and to also get English-speaking guides for places such as the Hermitage Museum, it completely enriches the experience when you delve into the history of Catherine the Great. If you have the time to do so, drive out to the Catherine Palace and Park if the weather is nice, as that is a beautiful building, too. It is about a 40-minute drive, and getting a private car is quite useful. Another tip I would recommend is to learn a little bit of Russian if you can, as in our experience, Russians do not speak English or are reluctant to unless they are part of the hotel or hospitality industry, so if you wanted to approach locals on the street for help on directions, it might be helpful to learn some basic phrases!

THE WORLD IS YOUR OYSTER

Church of the Savior on Spilled Blood. Saint Petersburg. Russia. 2016.

An Interlude

State Hermitage Museum. Saint Petersburg. Russia. 2016.

I am so grateful to have had this trip with my mother, as there were so many moments when if shared with anyone else, would not be as special. Now, looking towards the future, and how we are no longer living in the same country, it seems that these moments where it was just the two of us will now be quite sparse, so I'm really happy to have these incredible memories to look back on. Over the years, my mother and I have had a lot of time to bond, be it moving to Australia together just the two of us, or travelling to amazing countries such as this trip, and every moment counts, and I truly could not be luckier to have such a strong, caring, and loving mother by my side. She has been my role model since the day I was born, and she is the reason why I am forging my own path in the world now, following in her footsteps and becoming a doctor, too.

Turkey 2019

I hold such fond memories of this holiday, as it may be my favourite of them all thus far. At this point in my life, my partner and I had been doing long distance for almost a year and a half now, and I was living in the UK, having moved there in August 2018, and he was in Singapore for work.

THE WORLD IS YOUR OYSTER

One of the most exciting things about moving to the UK was that it really broadened the scope of places we could meet in between, much more so than what was in between Melbourne, Australia, and Singapore, and when we looked at the map, we were immediately drawn to Turkey, where East meets West, as the cliche saying goes.

We mostly agreed to plan together, with long skype calls where we disagreed on accommodation (there were so many cave suites to look at in Cappadocia), and discussions on what we would actually do during our limited time there, but to me, organising and planning is truly half, if not three-quarters of the fun. We also agreed to surprise each other with a birthday surprise, since we were unable to be together for our birthdays in March and April and our trip was planned for May. He ended up surprising me with an ATV ride through Rose Valley in Cappadocia, which is, and will always be one of the most special moments of my life, while I booked a street food tour in Istanbul, as we've started a tradition of going to food tours in every country we visit, to immerse ourselves within the culture and appreciate the place a little bit more. We still talk about these incredible experiences to this day, as it really left a mark in our memories.

My partner, Nihal and myself in Rose Valley, Cappadocia, Turkey, 2019.

An Interlude

The three cities we visited during our 10-day trip were Cappadocia, Izmir, and Istanbul. Most of our time was spent in Cappadocia and Istanbul, with Izmir as a filler city in between. My favourite was Cappadocia, as the natural rock formations were stunning, and there was so much to do. Cappadocia is the city where you see all the hot air balloon images from Turkey, and we were booked in to do a hot air balloon ride but unfortunately it was cancelled because the air pressure was too high and the hot air balloons would not have been able to rise, and that week alone was a clear indicator that it was not a good time for a hot air balloon ride, as the days leading up to our day had been cancelled, too. If you have an extra day to spare, after all the ATV riding and rock formation exploring, make sure to check out Goreme Open Air Museum, too, a UNESCO World Heritage Site. It is a museum of many rock-formed churches with stunning wall-paintings dating back to the 10th–12th centuries.

We were only in Izmir for two nights, and the sole reason why we decided to go there was because we wanted to see the ancient Greek city of Ephesus. We absolutely loved Ephesus, and highly recommend it if you ever decide to visit Turkey. We booked a private tour, which meant we had someone driving us to and from, and someone explaining all the little details to us, which was a wise decision. The highlight of Ephesus was the Celsus Library, and you have to see it for yourself to understand why. If you can, make sure to go early in the morning

Nihal and I in front of Celsus Library, Ephesus, Turkey, 2019.

to avoid crowds, and if you decide to purchase a museum pass, it is valid here, too. Our tour also took us to the House of Virgin Mary and the Temple of Artemis, which is worth seeing since you're already in the area.

I wasn't expecting to love Istanbul as much as I did. It's the capital city, so I thought it wouldn't be as fun as Cappadocia, and I thought it would be very touristy, and while it was at times, there is so much to do in Istanbul, that the five or so days we had were simply not enough. We managed to do the Hagia Sofia Museum, the Grand Bazaar and the Blue Mosque, but it felt like there was still so much to see. As mentioned before, we also did an amazing street food tour that really helped us appreciate Turkish food and the culture more, and we cannot recommend it enough. If you are like us, and really enjoy learning about and eating new and interesting foods, Turkey is absolutely the place to do a food tour. I ate so many things that I normally would not have dared to try, but if you are vegan or vegetarian, I noticed that a lot of their foods are meat-based or contains animal products, so that is one thing to be wary about. I particularly loved baklava and the doner kebabs. We also tried to go to a few highly rated restaurants, and really enjoyed our experience at Leb-i-Derya specifically. If you book in advance, hopefully you will get a table with a view, as the view is really lovely.

(L-R) Dolma. Baklava and Turkish Apple Tea. Turkey. 2019.

What I'm most grateful for from this trip is having a partner who loves travelling, too, who loves to explore new and wonderful cities with me, which I think would have been very difficult if he wasclose-minded. Travelling with your partner is such a fantastic way of seeing if you are actually compatible or not, and allows for your differing point of views to shine or collide, but it is a great way of allowing compromise into your relationship (as mentioned before), you are constantly working together to have the best trip possible.

An Interlude

This trip also helped us realise how in sync we can be with each other, allowing for things to progress very efficiently and smoothly, and that we have to always strive to be understanding and patient with one another. I remember there was one day, probably our second or so day in Turkey, we were in Cappadocia and had kept it a relaxing day as we were worried about jet lag (more so for him as he was coming from Singapore). We decided to go for a nice hike through love Valley, and it started off great. I was feeling pumped, excited to explore a new city, looking forward to amazing views, and then a few hours into it, it started to get quite hilly, the rocks were uneven, and then a few more hours after that, it felt like we were going nowhere and an exit out of the valley did not look promising. It was starting to get dark and I was nervous that we would get lost in unknown territory, and we came across another hiker who said, 'Oh you definitely won't get out before dark.' And I started panicking and getting scared. My amazing partner remained calm throughout (he's a seasoned hiker, too, which helped, unlike me), and slowly, very patiently guided us out of the valleys and we finally made it back to the hotel eight or so hours later, out of water and completely depleted of energy. I felt so accomplished after that hike, and looking back now, we can only laugh at how stressed I was at the time.

Final Thoughts

While these two trips have been my most memorable travels in recent times, for different reasons, I tend to look back on my holidays and think of distinct moments rather than an entire holiday as being the 'best'. Some other special memories I have had whilst travelling include going to Taipei, Taiwan with my partner and getting caught in a hurricane, so we spent our entire weekend indoors playing video games, or going to Da Nang, Vietnam for a New Year's weekend with two friends and because the weather was rainy the entire time, all we did was get massages and eat. Or that time the friend I travelled to New York City with and myself slept on the streets of New York for 30 hours or so to get tickets to a taping of *Saturday Night Live*. (Don't worry, Mum, there were other people lining up and sleeping, too, and we felt safe the entire time.). These are the moments that I constantly look back on, sometimes not believing that I ever did that, or just laughing to myself over how the weekend we had planned did not go according to plan at all. I believe you only ever get these memories from travelling, from exposing yourself to the world and making yourself vulnerable, and no matter how bizarre, how strange the experience may have been, it always ends up being a great story to tell at dinner parties, and I would never trade that experience for anything else.

Final, final thoughts: a brief letter to my mother

Dear Mum,

Thank you for letting me be a part of your book and for letting me tell part of my story. Thank you for guiding me through life, and for showing Shai Wan and me the wonders of the world and travelling from such a young age. I am grateful you have opened our eyes to this vast, beautiful place that I'll constantly want to explore. You have ignited in us a passion for the unknown, a passion for adventure with tales of your own travels, and I appreciate the fact that that love for travelling has not dwindled in your old age. If anything, your urge to explore has only increased as you have aged. Thank you for showing me how to stay grounded and humble, and for being the epitome of love, kindness and grace. Shai and I are so lucky to have you as our mother, and we will never forget it. I love you.

Love,
Kimberly

Chapter Six:
Preparation For Travel

To book flights, trains, cruises, hotel accommodations, and tours, you should consider your itinerary and desired destinations. You can book these services with travel agents, flight centers, cruise experiences, wilderness safaris, or book them yourself.

Travel Agents

Travel agents are useful for those who are working and do not have much time to search online or who prefer less hassle and want someone to arrange everything for them. Travel agents are also beneficial for people who have never traveled overseas before. However, it is important to note that travel agent staff may not always have extensive knowledge about traveling. While they may have traveled to a few countries in their time, they may not have worked in different countries or have had the time to build up their travel experience. Most of the knowledge they possess may come from online research.

Additionally, travel agents may subcontract some services, such as visa applications or train and cruise tours, to other companies. If you are traveling extensively for two-three months and taking an airplane to one or two countries before continuing your journey on a train or a cruise, it is important to be aware that the main travel agent you are booking may not have full control over these subcontracted tour agents. Problems can arise, such as delays in visa processing or errors in itinerary planning.

Booking Itineraries Yourself

For those who have traveled overseas a few times, it may be more convenient to book their own itineraries via online bookings or Google searches. Sometimes, airlines offer promotions on their websites, and you can also find ideas for your next trip while on your current one. For example, while on a world cruise for three weeks, I was encouraged by the cruise staff to book my next trips with them, and they offered discounts to entice passengers.

Booking itineraries yourself can also save you money as you can often find cheaper tickets than those offered by travel agents. Travel magazines and brochures can also be a good source of information for planning your travels.

Getting Information

When planning a trip, it is important to gather information about the country, city, and specific places you wish to visit. You can obtain this information from travel books, country-specific books, travel magazines, or the internet. Many younger people use websites such as TripAdvisor to research information and find suitable accommodations. It is also important to stay up to date with the latest news about the country or countries you plan to visit. This includes monitoring for wars, protests, fires, floods, hurricanes, earthquakes, and health outbreaks such as SARS, Ebola, Swine Flu, Bird Flu, MERS, Influenza, Dengue Fever, or Malaria. Additionally, some countries may be difficult or dangerous to travel to during certain periods, particularly if your country is in conflict with that country or if the relationship between the countries is unstable. In such cases, it is best to avoid traveling to that country altogether.

With the COVID-19 pandemic, many countries imposed lockdowns in 2020 and 2021, resulting in restricted travel. As of 2022, travel is once again possible, but it is important to follow all the rules and regulations, including having a fully COVID-19 vaccination certificate and undergoing PCR or RAT tests before travel. These requirements can change frequently, so it is essential to stay up to date with the latest information and comply with all the necessary guidelines. I advise travelers that, if they hear news of epidemics, pandemics, or wars while in a country or on a cruise ship, they should try to return home as soon as possible to avoid being locked in.

Private Tours

If your travel dates and times do not align with any available tour groups, you can book a private tour. You can find private tour guides through advertisements or by contacting private travel agents. Alternatively, you can book a private tour yourself. Private tours can make your trip special, as you can customize your itinerary and take detours based on your preferences. Your family, private tour guide, and driver will accompany you, so you do not have to worry about other people's schedules. In contrast, with tour groups, you must stick to the itinerary and cannot take detours.

Preparation For Travel

Visas

Visas are essential for traveling to many countries, especially in recent times. Applying for visas is more critical now than it was 35 to 40 years ago when I used to travel. If you plan to travel from one country to another and return again, you will need to apply for a multiple-entry visa. If you have limited time, it is best to apply for visas yourself, particularly in large countries where the capital city is far from your place of residence. You can find the embassies and foreign consulates' offices in the capital city.

If you cannot apply for a visa yourself, and you want the travel company to do it for you, you will need to provide them with more time. Some travel agents subcontract other companies to process visa applications, so be sure to check and apply yourself if you need it quickly.

Travel Agents

Travel agents are an excellent option if you are unsure how to book your itinerary. However, if you are an experienced traveler and have enough time, it is best to book it yourself. In some cases, you can still ask travel agents for recommendations on what to do or which tours to book.

Insurance

Travel insurance is crucial, covering unlimited medical and dental emergencies, 24/7 assistance, lost luggage, bags, or handbags stolen, and more. The price of the coverage depends on the type of cover you take, with disaster cover being the most expensive option. In my 40 years of traveling, I have only had to make three claims. Once, an airport personnel mistakenly sent my luggage to another city in Mexico, and it arrived the following day, with no claim paid out. I had to wear my spare clothes in my overnight bag for the night and the next day. It is always good to carry a light overnight bag with a set of clothes, toiletries, and your usual medications.

Another time, my handbag was stolen at the railway station in a big city in a European country. We searched for a police station for two hours, and I only received compensation for my phone and camera after producing a police report. My mobile phone served as evidence that I used it in that country, as I mentioned it was in my handbag. A month later, I received some money back. Lastly, I missed a flight in South Africa due to heavy traffic. I arrived at the counter 45 minutes before departure, but they refused to allow me on the plane. I was able to take the next flight two days later with the same airline.

Money: How to Carry It with You

When traveling, it's important to have money to pay for tours, food, souvenirs, shopping, and other expenses, even if you've already paid for your tickets, flights, cruises, and accommodations. Credit cards are a useful option, especially travel cards like Cash Passport, which can be loaded with money in multiple currencies and used like a credit card. This is safer than carrying a large amount of cash. However, in some countries and remote areas, cash is still the easiest and sometimes the only accepted payment method. For example, when traveling in remote areas in India, Cambodia, Mexico, and Africa, I found that cash was necessary. Some countries even prefer US dollars, UK pounds, or euros over their own currency. In addition, some taxis and businesses in Asian countries may not accept credit cards. During the Covid-19 pandemic, many countries have also begun accepting cards only, making it even more important to have a credit card.

Things to Buy Before You Travel

Depending on your destination, season, and climate, appropriate clothing is essential. For example, if you're traveling to a cold winter climate with snow and ice, you should bring warm coats, snow boots, and gloves. I once traveled to Warsaw in winter without appropriate winter gear, and it was -14 degrees and icy. We had to buy clothes and gear at a store. Another time, when I went to Norway in February 2016, we visited Finland and St. Petersburg where the winter snow and temperatures dropped to -8/-10 degrees. On a ship from Bergen to Northern Norway, I was not appropriately dressed, but a kind lady noticed and lent me her extra coat, socks, gloves, and beanie. It's always helpful to pack appropriately for the climate you'll be experiencing. If you're traveling during the summer, light cotton clothing, sunscreen, hats, and seaside swimwear are essential, as well as Bermuda shorts and umbrellas.

What to Pack in your Luggage or Hand Luggage?

The weight allowance and luggage policy depend on the airline you book with. For instance, budget or luxury airlines, First Class, Business Class, or Economy Class may offer 20kg or 30kg weight allowance and a different number of luggages you can carry. Most hand luggages have a weight limit of approximately 7 kg and a size limit.

It's advisable to pack your clothes in your main luggage, and if you have any liquid bottles or perfumes, they must be checked in. Small scissors and nail cutters should also be in the main luggage. In contrast, your hand luggage should not contain any liquids 100 ml or over or sharp objects.

Preparation For Travel

However, it's recommended to keep a clean set of clothes in your hand luggage in case your luggage gets lost. In 1984, when the airline lost my luggage before my three-month stint in Mexico, they told me I was on an earlier plane (when I was obviously not) and advised me to continue my bus journey. I insisted on waiting for my luggage in Marzatlan if they provided a hotel for a night, but they refused. Fortunately, I had packed toiletries and a set of clothes in my hand luggage, which I used for my night in the Mexican village. The next day, my luggage arrived at the village where I was staying.

When travelling on luxury trains for a few days, the cabins may be small, and the luggage you can bring on board may have size restrictions. Most overnight trains have limited space for larger baggage, which is stored in the luggage compartments. However, if the train is a luxury suite, you may be able to bring in bigger luggage, depending on the available space. In general, normal-sized train cabins only allow smaller bags to avoid limiting your movement inside the cabin.

Travel Tips:

1. Pack your own luggage.
2. Never carry anything out of your country for someone else.
3. Never leave your luggage unattended at airports.
4. Make copies of your passport, itinerary, tickets, and visas, and leave them with someone at home.
5. Respect local laws, rules, and customs.
6. See a doctor or travel specialist about necessary vaccines for yourself and the countries you're visiting.

What to do on the Plane/Flight:

1. Move your toes and feet every 15 to 20 minutes while sitting.
2. Get up and walk around every 2 hours or so.
3. Stay hydrated by drinking water and juice.
4. On long flights, watch movies or sleep with an eye mask and noise-cancelling headphones.

Upon Arrival at the Airport:

Before arriving, some airlines will inform you on their mini TV screens which luggage claim to go to. Use travel apps to stay updated on flight information. Remember to have your mobile phone with you, and stay aware of new technologies and facilities.

Chapter Seven:
Health Issues and Prevention

Before traveling, it's important to see your doctor (GP) for a medical check-up and advice to ensure you're physically and mentally fit, prevent infections, and have a safe and enjoyable trip. The physical check-up should include a general check-up, physical examination, chest, lungs, heart, blood pressure, abdomen, and limbs depending on the person's age. It's also good to have general check-up blood tests like fasting glucose, Hb A1C, fasting cholesterol, triglycerides, liver function tests, kidney, and thyroid function tests. However, if you're seeing your usual doctor who knows you and has done general check-ups before, you may not need to do these tests. If your GP is not confident to give advice on travel-related health issues, you should see a doctor who is an expert in Travel Medicine or visit a Travel Clinic.

When you inform your doctor that you're traveling, the first thing they'll ask is whether you're up to date with your vaccines, such as your flu vaccine or tetanus vaccine. The next step is to determine which country or countries you're visiting and the vaccines required, which may include hepatitis A vaccine, typhoid vaccine, rabies vaccine, yellow fever vaccine, Japanese encephalitis vaccine, and prevention of cholera or traveller's diarrhoea, as well as prevention of malaria.

If you're traveling to many developing countries for the first time, it's recommended to get hepatitis A and typhoid vaccines. Hepatitis A vaccine requires two doses, and the typhoid vaccine can be administered orally or by injection. The oral vaccine, Vivotif, requires three oral capsules taken on days 1, 3, and 5. The oral doses must be taken one week before travel. Vivotif oral provides 71% protective efficacy in one year, with sustained protection of 67% provided over three years. The injection vaccine, Typhim, lasts for three years after one dose.

For cholera prevention, it's recommended to take Dukoral oral vaccine, which also prevents traveller's diarrhoea. Malaria prevention is also important for travelers visiting many countries. Some areas in Cambodia and remote areas as well as safaris require malaria prevention measures. When traveling to malarious areas, it's important to take anti-malarial tablets, use anti-mosquito repellents, and wear long-sleeve blouses and trousers, preferably in light colors as mosquitoes are attracted to black clothing.

For malaria prevention, you will need antimalarial tablets, specifically doxycycline 100 mg once daily. Start taking one or two days before traveling and continue daily after returning from the malaria area for about three to four weeks. This medication can be given to individuals above eight years old. Lariam is also an option and should be taken one tablet weekly, starting a week before travel, continuing throughout the stay, and for one week after returning.

There is now another vaccine available to prevent malaria called Kodatef or tefenoquine (as succinate). This vaccine is for G6PD normal individuals and protects against *P. vivax*, *P. falciparum*, and *P. ovale*. Kodatef provides 99.1% prophylactic protection against *P. vivax* infection. This vaccine is only given to individuals aged 18 years and above and is administered weekly.

Yellow fever vaccine is necessary for travel to some African and South American countries. You need a certificate indicating that you have received the yellow fever vaccine if you have traveled to these countries and wish to return to your home country or other countries.

Rabies vaccine is needed when traveling to remote areas for work or holiday, or when volunteering in large countries such as India, China, and Africa where there are stray dogs and limited access to hospitals and medical clinics. It is important to weigh the risks and benefits of this vaccine, as it can have adverse side effects. However, the new rabies vaccine has very few side effects compared to older versions.

For instance, when I was doing my master's degree in Maternal and Child Health at the University of London in 1981, I traveled to India and received the rabies vaccine before leaving the UK. The area where I was staying had a lot of stray dogs, and the nearest hospital was 28 kilometers away. The vaccine was recommended by my doctor due to the high risk and need for prevention.

I recently had a patient, a young lady planning to travel to several Southeast Asian countries to save stray dogs. During her health check and vaccinations, it was determined that she needed hepatitis A, typhoid, and rabies vaccines (doses 1, 2, and 3) before traveling. The rabies vaccine produced today has very few side effects compared to the one I received years ago.

The Japanese encephalitis vaccine is used to prevent a rare viral brain infection that spreads through mosquitoes. It is most common in rural areas of South East Asia, the Pacific Islands, and the Far East. Although it is rare for short-term travelers to contract the virus, those traveling for a month or longer in endemic countries or frequent travelers to endemic areas should consider getting the vaccine, which is known as the JE Spect vaccine. While it can be expensive, it may be worth it for peace of mind.

In addition to Japanese encephalitis, there are several other medical conditions and health issues that travelers may encounter. These include fever, gastroenteritis, vomiting, diarrhoea, and skin rashes. To avoid foodborne illness, it's recommended to boil, cook, or peel food, or forget it altogether.

Travelers with chronic medical conditions such as diabetes mellitus, bronchial asthma, chronic obstructive pulmonary disease, and heart disease should have a medical check-up with their doctors before traveling and carry a health summary and list of medications they are taking.

Travelers with allergies, including food allergies, should inform airline staff of their allergies and avoid airplane food if possible. Those who have had anaphylaxis should carry an EpiPen and a letter from their GP as airports will check. Motion sickness can be prevented with medications from a GP or purchased on a cruise ship.

Pregnant women should not travel during the first trimester of pregnancy, up to 12 weeks. Airlines will also not allow pregnant women who are 36 weeks or more to fly. Traveling with young children can be enjoyable, although they may experience ear discomfort during takeoff and landing. Parents traveling with babies may have access to extra leg space and a rectangular bed for their child to sleep in.

Long Flights

During long flights such as from New York, USA to Australia, I have had patients who developed Deep Vein Thrombosis. Some people remain seated and do not move for extended periods, causing the condition. To prevent this, I recommend getting up and walking to the back of the airplane every two to three hours, going to the restroom, and moving your legs.

For flights such as from Singapore to London, which take about 13 to 14 hours, it is also advisable to move about and stretch your legs.

Fear of Flying

For individuals who are scared of flying, doctors can prescribe a few tablets of Valium. One tablet should be taken just before traveling to calm the person down. Before the Covid pandemic, Qantas conducted a training program to help people who were afraid of flying. A young woman who was previously scared of even short trips within Australia took the training lesson at Qantas and reported feeling more at ease.

Health Issues and Prevention

Preventing Infections

Epidemics, pandemics, and infections are constantly changing and affecting different countries. Some countries are experiencing epidemics such as malaria, ebola, dengue fever, and influenza, while the Covid pandemic has affected the entire world. Therefore, it is essential to stay updated on the latest news and discuss any travel plans with your doctor.

During my time working in Singapore in 2003, the SARS epidemic occurred, and it lasted about four to five months. Unfortunately, some health workers and doctors lost their lives. Although it was a severe condition, it did not spread much and was luckily short-lived.

Recently, while working in Australia, the Covid-19 coronavirus outbreak began, just like SARS, originating from China. The virus spread quickly and became a pandemic. Symptoms include cold and cough, flu-like symptoms, headaches, and fever. Traveling on planes, trains, coaches, cruise ships, and enclosed areas can cause infections to spread easily. In March 2020, several cruise ships stopped in Sydney Port, and many people on board tested positive for Covid-19. As people are in close proximity in cruise ships for several weeks or months, infections can spread easily. Influenza and gastroenteritis also commonly occur on cruise ships. It is essential to take necessary precautions and avoid enclosed areas with crowds.

Tips for Pre-Travel Preparation

1. Ensure physical and mental fitness.
2. Get pre-travel vaccines depending on the destination.
3. Stomach and bowel problems are common during travel. Experts advise boiling, peeling, cooking food or not eating it. Carry a first aid kit and oral rehydration sachets.
4. Carry usual medications and a letter from your GP if carrying Epipen Inj for anaphylaxis.
5. Use insect repellents with DEET and sleep under a mosquito net in malaria areas. Take anti-malarial tablets.
6. Abstain from casual sex or use a condom.
7. Avoid driving in unfamiliar areas, especially at night.
8. Ensure personal safety by carrying a neck and shoulder carry-on bag with passport, credit cards, cash, and mobile phone.
9. Obtain medical and travel insurance.
10. Credit cards are important during the Covid pandemic as many places only accept cards. Consider using a travel cash passport card.
11. Make copies of important documents and leave them with a family member at home.

Travelling During the Covid Pandemic

Travel during the Covid pandemic was difficult due to lockdowns. Even essential workers could not move freely. It is important to stay updated on the latest news as different countries have varying travel restrictions and requirements for vaccination.

Chapter Eight:
Miscellaneous

Exploring Different Countries' Cuisines

When visiting a different country, it is important to try their local cuisine to experience the original, authentic taste. Although you may have tried the same dishes in other countries or even in your home country, the taste may differ from the original. For instance, I learned this lesson while in Italy when a restaurant staff member informed me that their pizza and pasta tasted different from done in other countries. Eat here this is original! He said.

In this chapter, I will highlight some of the famous dishes from a few countries that hold a special place in my life.

Singapore

    a. **Hainanese Chicken Rice:** This is a national dish that consists of poached chicken served with white rice, soy sauce, chili garlic dip, and pickled young ginger. The dish was created by immigrants from Hainan, Southern China, and is found in most eateries in Singapore.

    b. **Hokkien Mee:** This dish is made by frying yellow noodles with prawns and squid, served with chili and lime.

    c. **Chilli Crab:** This is a signature seafood dish in Singapore, featuring hard-shelled crabs cooked with shallots, garlic, ginger, chili, and cornstarch.

    d. **Wonton Noodle Soup:** This dish consists of wonton dumplings, thin yellow noodles, and chicken soup, and is filled with ingredients like minced pork, roughly chopped prawns, chicken, shallots, garlic, and ginger.

    e. **Fish Head Curry:** This dish features a fish head cut in half, cooked with oil, onion, garlic, chili powder, turmeric powder, coriander powder, salt, eggplant, and ladyfingers.

    f. **Char Kway Teow:** This is a popular street food made of flat rice noodles stir-fried with shrimp, bean sprouts, chives, and Chinese sausage.

    g. **Chee Cheong Fun:** This dish is made of steamed rice noodle rolls with soy sauce and chili paste.

THE WORLD IS YOUR OYSTER

    h. **Chwee Kueh:** This dish is a type of steamed rice cake served with spicy preserved radish.
    i. **Hor Fun:** This dish consists of wide rice noodles stir-fried with vegetables and meats.
    j. **Carrot Cake:** This dish is made of stir-fried white radish cake with eggs, garlic, and preserved radish.
    k. **Spring Rolls:** This dish can be vegetarian or made with prawns or minced pork.
    l. **Old Chang Kee Curry Puff:** This famous curry puff is made with chicken, potato, egg, onion, garlic, and mild spices.
    m. **Dim Sum:** This Cantonese cuisine features small plates of dumplings and other snack dishes, enjoyed with tea.

Some of the popular dim sum dishes include:
1. **Xiu mai:** Minced pork or shrimp wrapped in a cup-shaped wrapper with mushrooms and water chestnuts.
2. **Xiaolong bao:** Soup dumplings filled with hot broth and pork.
3. **BBQ Pork Buns:** White bread buns stuffed with barbecued seasoned pork.
4. **Chicken Feet:** Deep-fried chicken feet braised in a sweet fermented black bean sauce.
5. **Cheong Fun:** Handmade steamed rice noodles rolled with shrimp or minced meat.
6. **Spring Rolls:** Vegetarian or with chicken.
7. **Dessert - Egg Tart:** Sweet, custard-filled flaky tartlets that originated from Macau. The Singapore Sling at Raffles Hotel is also a must-try drink.

Malaysia

    a. **Laksa**
        Laksa is a spicy noodle dish popular in Southeast Asia. It consists of various types of noodles with toppings of chicken, prawn or fish, prepared with a rich and spicy coconut soup or broth, tamarind, and spices. It was created by Peranakans.
    b. Mee Goreng
    c. Nasi Padang
        Very famous and popular in Malaysia.
    d. Nasi Lemak

This dish features rice cooked in coconut milk with fried chicken or fried dried anchovies, peanuts, cucumber slices, onion and garlic sambal paste, and boiled egg.

MISCELLANEOUS

Myanmar (Burma)

a. Ohn Noh Kauk Swe (Coconut Noodle dish)
b. Moh Hin Gah (Fish Vermicelli dish)
c. Let Thoke (Salad Mixture)
d. Toh Fu Nway (Shan Toh Foo)
   This is a popular Shan dish with yellow noodles or rice noodles with sliced chicken or minced pork fried with onions and garlic, paprika or chilies, pounded peanuts, and preserved mustard or sliced preserved small cucumber with soft tofu paste on top of noodles.
e. Toh Fu Fried
   This is when Toh Fu paste is not soft and stirred on fire, then put in a container.
f. Green Mango Salad/Let Thoke
h. La Phet Thoke (Pickled Tea leaves with a mixture of nuts)
i. Gin Thoke (Pickled young ginger with a mixture of nuts)
j. Pei Pyote (Steamed peas)
k. See Pyan Hin (Oil curry dishes of fish, chicken, mutton)
i. Chin Yei Hin (Sour taste with vegetables like gourd, green papaya or with "Ga Zun Ywet" with onions, garlic, chilies, fish sauce, and tamarind)
j. Belly pork with soy sauce and mushrooms
k. Hta Ma Nei (Glutinous rice with coconut milk, grated coconuts, sesame seeds, and peanuts)
l. Kha Yan Thee Hnat (Eggplant with oil, onions, garlic, chilies, dried prawns pounded with fish sauce)
m. Ma Yan Thee Thoke (Salad)

Snacks:

1. Boo Thee Gyaw (Fried Gourd)
2. Ba Yar Gyaw (Fried peas)
3. Pork fritters (Shan snacks, pork, mushroom, spring onions mixed with rice flour, slight glutinous flour, salt, and fried)
4. Ah Loo Gyaw (Fried potato)

Desserts:

1. Shwe Yin Aye (Sago, coconut milk)
2. Kyawk Kyaw (Burmese coconut dessert)

3. Sanwin Makin (Burmese semolina cake)
4. Mok Lone Yay Baw (Burmese sticky rice balls)

Japan

Tempura: fried fish and vegetables
Sushi: Japanese sushi rice with salmon, eel, prawns, and other ingredients
Japanese Ramen: noodles
Japanese rice crackers
Eel dishes

United Kingdom

Fish and chips

Yorkshire pudding: a crispy pastry that can be eaten with sausages, chicken roast, or other meats, along with potatoes and vegetables
Roast chicken, roast pork, roast beef

Soups

BBQ meats and veggies
Salads
Hungary
Goulash soup

China

Peking Duck: available in different styles
Noodles: different types
Roast pork, Char Siew, belly pork, and roast duck are usually found in the same stall
Congee (rice porridge): can be served with chicken, pork, or fish, and usually eaten with Yu chow kway
Fried vegetables: available in different varieties
Steamed pork bun with egg and mushroom, Char Suei Bun
Egg Tarts
Dumplings

MISCELLANEOUS

India

Biryani: chicken with spices and rice or with lamb
Paratha and Naan: can be eaten with chicken curry or with pea or lentil soups
Samosa: fried vegetarian or with meat, Pappadom: crispy crackers

Cambodia

   a. Na Tang: crispy rice with dipping sauce
   b. Nhoam Mi Suor: a chicken vermicelli salad
   c. Num Banh Chok Ka Ri: rice noodles served in chicken curry
   d. Rice puff crackers
   e. Deep-fried sticky rice crackers

Theatres, Art, Music Museums

It is also enjoyable to visit the world's famous places like the theatres in London. During my stay in London from 1981 to 1983, I saw several theatre shows, including *Mary Poppins*, *The Sound of Music*, and *The King and I*. I also saw famous actors and actresses like Yul Bruner and Julie Andrews.

In the USA, Broadway shows in New York are worth visiting. I saw the *Chicago Musical* on Broadway during my stay in New York.

In Milan, "The Last Supper" is painted on the wall, so it can only be seen by visiting Milan. In France, the *Moulin Rouge* is a beautiful show.

There are also famous museums in different countries, such as the Museum at St Petersburg, the Louvre in Paris, and the Parliament building in Budapest.

Chapter Nine:
My Personal Experience of Different Countries and What I Still Want To Do

Over the years of traveling, I have seen how countries have changed, and there are some places that I cannot see anymore, like one of the Seven Natural Wonders and a few places that I have been to, like The Berlin Wall and Nepal Temples before the Earthquake, which are now gone. As a young traveler and now an older one, my desire for where I want to go and what I want to see has also changed. Sometimes what I thought of and later found out were very different.

I have seen many waterfalls, from young in Burma, to overseas Niagara Falls on the Canadian side in the early 1980s, and later on the USA side in 2018, in Australia, Darwin, and in Mauritius. One of my dream destinations, Victoria Falls, I saw both sides in Zambia and Zimbabwe. It was very beautiful and amazing, one of the Natural World Wonders. Victoria Falls is very big, and the waterfalls are magnificent. The Zambezi River flows, and then the waterfalls in Zambia and Zimbabwe on both sides. There is a bridge in between. I stayed in both countries and walked on the bridge. While I was on the bridge, I saw the waterfalls on both sides and even a rainbow. After seeing Victoria Falls, I never thought any other waterfall would be more beautiful, but I was wrong. I went to Laos with my daughter and visited Luang Prabang, a World Heritage site city. We visited 6 places including the Royal Palace Museum, the Night Market, Mekong River cruise and one of the two Waterfalls in Luang Prabang. We even went up the rocks to another cave where beautiful weaving was done, and I missed the chance to buy some because I didn't have the local currency.

When you visit remote areas in a country, it is good to have the local currency as some places may not accept foreign currency or credit cards. After we visited those places, we still had three more days left, and I suggested we visit Kuang Si Fall, a bigger waterfall. It was about one and a half hours from our hotel on the bank of Mekong River. We hired a van for the whole trip, and we were amazed by the beauty of the waterfall. The water flowed down from the upper rocks, and the water picture looked like lace, and there were lagoons below. My daughter even swam in one of the lagoons.

My Personal Experience of Different Countries and What I Still Want To Do

There is never only one best or perfect country as all countries around the world have very different landscapes, architecture, and natural beauty. Only when you have visited many countries can you know about it. Some people who have never traveled or have only visited one or two countries always say their country is the best, but it is not correct as no country has everything.

As I am getting older, I may not be able to climb or walk a lot, but I still want to visit the countries that I have visited before and some countries that I have not visited yet. The countries that I have visited before will be very different, and even some that I have visited many times after a few years, they change. For example, when I visited Bodh Gaya, where Lord Buddha got enlightenment, in India in 1980/1981, the Bodhi tree was not enclosed, and there were very few people in that place. But when I went there again in 2015, it was packed with people coming in groups from different South East Asian countries.

Chapter Ten: Summary

1. "The world is your oyster" means you can do anything or go anywhere you want to. It's a great opportunity for younger people who have a lot of possibilities ahead of them.
2. All countries and places are beautiful in their own unique ways, with different landscapes, climates, and cultures. It's worthwhile to visit as many as you can.
3. When visiting other countries, it's important to show respect for the people and follow the local rules and customs.
4. Different modes of transportation can be used depending on where you are going and what you are doing.
5. Avoid traveling during times of natural disasters, such as earthquakes, floods, and wars, or when protests are happening.
6. Always remember to have your passport, visas, and travel insurance in order.
7. Visit your doctor, either a general practitioner or a travel specialist, to get immunizations, advice on medical conditions, medications, and any necessary documentation.
8. Different countries have different climates and seasons, so make sure you pack appropriate clothing for the weather.
9. It's a good idea to pack a set of clothes and some essential items, such as medication and toiletries, in your carry-on bag in case your luggage is lost or misplaced by the airline.
10. While traveling is exciting, it's also important to balance it with your education and career.

Shirley and Kimberly are happy to share their experiences with traveling and offer these tips to help make your journey happy, healthy, and safe. Bon voyage!